David Bowie
THE RISE AND FALL OF ZIGGY STARDUST AND THE SPIDERS FROM MARS

Laura Shenton

David Bowie
THE RISE AND FALL OF ZIGGY STARDUST AND THE SPIDERS FROM MARS

Laura Shenton

WP
WYMER
PUBLISHING
Bedford, England

First published in 2022 by Wymer Publishing
Bedford, England www.wymerpublishing.co.uk Tel: 01234 326691
Wymer Publishing is a trading name of Wymer (UK) Ltd

Copyright © 2022 Laura Shenton / Wymer Publishing. This edition published 2022.

Print edition (fully illustrated): **ISBN: 978-1-912782-92-5**

Edited by Jerry Bloom.

The Author hereby asserts her rights to be identified
as the author of this work in accordance with sections
77 to 78 of the Copyright, Designs & Patents Act 1988.

All rights reserved. No part of this publication may be
reproduced or transmitted in any form or by any means,
electronic or mechanical, including photocopying, or any
information storage and retrieval system, without written
permission from the publisher.

This publication is sold subject to the condition that it shall not,
by way of trade or otherwise, be lent, re-sold, hired out or
otherwise circulated without the publishers' prior consent in any
form of binding or cover other than that in which it is published
and without a similar condition including this condition
being imposed on the subsequent purchaser.

eBook formatting by Coinlea.
Printed and bound in Great Britain by
CMP, Dorset.

A catalogue record for this book is available from the British Library.

Typeset by Andy Bishop / 1016 Sarpsborg
Cover design by 1016 Sarpsborg.

Contents

Preface — 7

Chapter One: *Why The Rise And Fall Of Ziggy Stardust?* — 9

Chapter Two: *The Making Of* — 25

Chapter Three: *Live Performances* — 55

Chapter Four: *A Legacy* — 85

Discography — 104

Tour Dates — 109

"An audience appreciation is only going to be periodic at the best of times. You will fall in and out of favour continually. I do not think it should be something one should be looking for. You should turn around at the end of the day and say 'I really like that piece of work', or 'that piece of work sucked'. Not, 'was that popular or wasn't it popular?'"

- David Bowie (1987)

Preface

This is not the first book out there on David Bowie and I am certain that it won't be the last. Considering his phenomenal contribution to music and the arts in general, I'm willing to bet that there will always be more research and perspectives to come, and rightly so. Where does this book sit in such canon, you might ask? Well, it's pretty much what it says it is on the cover really: a detailed exploration into Bowie's *The Rise And Fall Of Ziggy Stardust And The Spiders From Mars* album — in terms of how it came to be and of the content and context surrounding it.

Throughout this book, you will see a culmination of many vintage resources. Maybe some will be familiar to you, maybe some will be new to you. Either way, I have keenly included them because one day, such things might become harder to source. I feel strongly that it is important to collate them in order to be able to offer an objective narrative.

In the interest of transparency, I have had no affiliation with David Bowie or with any of his associates. This book is based on extensive research and relevant commentary.

Chapter One

Why The Rise And Fall Of Ziggy Stardust?

The *Rise And Fall Of Ziggy Stardust And The Spiders From Mars* (often shortened to simply, *Ziggy Stardust*) is the fifth studio album by David Bowie. Released by RCA Records in the UK in June 1972, it was produced by Bowie and Ken Scott. It features Bowie's backing band, the Spiders From Mars: Mick Ronson on guitar, Trevor Bolder on bass and Mick Woodmansey on drums.

As is often the case for many commercially successful albums, *Ziggy Stardust* had a broad appeal. *Beat Instrumental* predicted in August 1972; "He's able to capture both the intellectual and emotional markets. Teeny fans will be happy to bop along and see what gear he's wearing this week whereas university audiences will begin compiling theses on "The Reflections of Contemporary Culture in the Work of David Bowie". For this reason, and also because I feel he's the best solo artist performing today, I'm willing to stick my pen out and predict he'll be the world's best in, let's say, November 1973."

Acknowledging the record's potential appeal with a teen audience whilst advocating highly of the creative charisma in the music overall, *Record World* considered in May 1972; "Having put Boston, Memphis, and other unlikely repositories of Martian sensibility though any number of ch-ch-ch-changes with his single of the same name as extracted from the long playing masterpiece that is *Hunky Dory*, David Bowie, re-coifed, spiky, acerbic, and salacious, has thrown his assault on the rock pantheon into high gear with the release of the splendid teentune, 'Starman', and a highly energetic fable for our times soon to be admired by one and all as his fifth album, *The Rise And Fall Of Ziggy Stardust And The Spiders From Mars* in which it is melodramatically revealed that rock and roll is fatal if followed to its logical conclusions."

"That Ziggy Stardust, who plies his trade in the last five years earth has to shake, rattle and roll, is a quite adorably treacherous mutation of the forms of charisma engendered by Mick Jagger, Marc Bolan, and Alice Cooper. And finally that any album with titles like 'Moonage Daydream', 'Suffragette City', and 'Soul Love' cannot be other than psyche-expanding in the extreme."

"As an extra added attraction, the Bowie-band is now about to be fixed in the annals of killer trios, and comprised of Mick Ronson on guitar, Trevor Bolder on bass, and Mick Woodmansey – better known as Woody Woodmansey – on drums, a Spiders tour is shaping up as a consummation devoutly to be wished. And what news story would be complete without the addendum that *Ziggy Stardust* is available on disc, stereo eight cartridge tape, and stereo cassette from RCA Victor, where one hopes David Bowie will work his show with increasing regularity."

In the August 1972 press kit that RCA issued in America, Bowie was introduced as follows: "David Bowie has come to the forefront of the new music of the new image seventies. His move to RCA Records resulted in the highly acclaimed *Hunky Dory* album, which received unprecedented critical huzzas... at least unprecedented until the release of Bowie's *The Rise And Fall Of Ziggy Stardust And The Spiders From Mars*, an album that has elicited such quotable quotes as 'A stunning work of genius' (*Circus*), 'A strong, moving, powerful piece of rock and roll' (*LA Times*), 'The Elvis of the seventies' (Lillian Roxon of the *N.Y. News*) and 'David Bowie is one bitch of a rocker' (Ron Ross in *Words & Music*). And too, there is the interesting prognostication of Nancy Erlich in the *N.Y. Times*: 'The day will come when David Bowie is a star and the crushed remains of his melodies are broadcast from muzak boxes in every elevator and hotel lobby in town'."

"In an interview in *Rolling Stone*, Bowie has explained himself and his attitude toward his music (explaining himself is a thing he is frequently called upon to do). 'What the music says may be serious,' he says, 'but as a medium it should not be questioned, analysed or taken too seriously. I think it should be tarted up, made into a prostitute, a parody of itself. It should be the clown, the Pierrot medium. The music is the mask the message wears — music is the Pierrot and I, the performer, am the message'."

"In 1972, David Bowie — with his supercharged band The Spiders From Mars — began a series of gigs in the United Kingdom and the United States. It has been a while since the hyper-kinetic Bowie has been seen on stage, and the audience response has been a killer. One UK writer describes the Bowie phenom like this: 'Bowie… dressed first as Harlequin meets Star Trek, and then in Garboesque white satin. He has a painted white face, a haircut from *Clockwork Orange* and moves like a marionette. For the next few months his picture will be in every magazine. And yet — amazingly enough — he is a remarkable performer'."

"And in *Disc*, *Ziggy Stardust* gets this accolade: 'The music stands up on its own as some of the best rock to arrive on our minds for years.' David Bowie has often been described as the darling of the avant-garde, but now it has become clear that he has moved into the greater arena now and his impact is overall invading areas previously thought the property of the 'Puppy Love' school of music, and too, shaking up the ears of the rock purists. David Bowie will go where he wishes to go — as he always has. Armed with his two RCA Records albums and his

David Bowie - *The Rise And Fall Of Ziggy Stardust*

phenomenal band, it is certainly likely that, to quote *Words & Music*, 'David and company... will kick more sonic ass than any group since the Stones.' And what does David Bowie say? 'Look out you rock and rollers...' That's what he says."

The press kit introduced The Spiders From Mars:

"Mick Ronson: Played in a number of regional bands including two and a half years with The Crestas. Went to London and along with starving played with a band called Voice. Left that band and worked in a garage before joining doomed band called Wanted. Great debt and undernourishment. Worked at various day-labour jobs, joined Rats, and went with them to France where tour floundered, management snafued. Returned to London, got thrown out by family, re-joined Rats, and worked as gardener at girls' school. Broke even financially and joined David Bowie as lead guitar and arranger. Masterfully arranges much of Bowie repertory."

"Mick Woodmansey: Born in Driffield, England, and began drumming at the age of five. Started his own group at fifteen; performed locally. Joined Roadrunners and played with them for three years, and then joined Mick Ronson in Rats. Later played in a band called Ronno with Ronson and Trevor Bolder. Split Ronno and returned to London. Joined David Bowie."

"Trevor Bolder: Learned the trumpet from his father at age nine. Became cornet soloist with school band for three years. Began playing bass guitar, and with brother, formed Chicago Star Blues Band. Worked with various bands (Jelly Roll, Flesh) and then took some time off. Joined Ronno with Ronson and Woodmansey. All joined David Bowie. Trevor has worked as a decorator, a hairdresser and a piano tuner. And that is the Spider Web."

Why The Rise And Fall Of Ziggy Stardust?

Described by some as a rock opera and by many a loose concept album, *Ziggy Stardust* concerns Bowie's titular alter ego Ziggy Stardust. Stardust is a fictional rock star, sent to Earth as a saviour prior to an impending apocalyptic disaster. The character was an amalgamation of multiple inspirations, some of which Bowie was candid about, others that the media at the time liberally promoted as fact. The majority of the album's themes were determined by the songs chosen for the final cut after recording. The character featured on the tour that followed the release of the album. Bowie said of Ziggy in 1987; "He was half out of sci-fi rock and half out of the Japanese theatre. The clothes were, at that time, simply outrageous. And simply, nobody had seen anything like them before."

Ziggy Stardust wasn't Bowie's first delve into the concept of rock opera. In 1968, he had worked with Ken Pitt (his manager at the time) on a sequence called 'Ernie Johnson'. Thematically, the project was bizarre and trippy. It featured a story in which, at the end, the title character commits suicide. Of course, is Ziggy Stardust actually a rock opera? Comparatively, it is more likely that it was a cluster of iconic ideas put together into a sequence. Essentially, so many songs were recorded for what would become the *Ziggy Stardust* album that really, the character of Ziggy Stardust was to become an alter ego for Bowie pretty much at the last minute. Importantly though, the concept worked. The Stardust name was chosen in reference to the 'Legendary Stardust Cowboy', a song by Hoagy Carmichael. Bowie said in later years that the idea for Ziggy Stardust came to him in a dream.

The songs on *Ziggy Stardust* are indicative of a fascinating blend of influences; Iggy Pop of the Stooges, Lou Reed of the Velvet Underground, and Marc Bolan of T. Rex. The lyrics explore the superficial nature of rock music, stardom, sexuality, politics, and drug use.

In the UK, *Ziggy Stardust* peaked at number five. In the US, it got to number seventy-five on the US *Billboard* 200. Importantly though, it was the album that propelled Bowie to stardom in both. In the first week of its release, it entered the UK charts at a comfortable number nineteen. Not only that, but it sold 8,000 copies in the first week — a huge number for an artist of Bowie's stature at the time. It would go on to spend a total of 172 weeks in the UK chart.

****

Following a promotional tour of America in February 1971, Bowie was back in the UK. At the time he was living at Haddon Hall, a sprawling Victorian villa in Beckenham, south London, where he lived with his wife Angie and an assortment of musicians. The couple rented a ground-floor flat for £7 a week. It was here where he started working on songs inspired by the diversity of music that he had come across whilst in the US. Previously, he had composed on the acoustic guitar but at Haddon Hall, he used the piano. During this time, he wrote at least thirty songs. Many of them would go on to appear on his fourth studio album, *Hunky Dory* and indeed his fifth, *Ziggy Stardust*. Amongst the list were 'Hang On To Yourself' and 'Moonage Daydream'. He recorded both songs with his short-lived band Arnold Corns but of course, they would be re-recorded for the *Ziggy Stardust* album.

Work on what was to become the *Hunky Dory* album began officially in June 1971 at London's Trident Studios. Present at the sessions were the musicians who would later come to be called The Spiders From Mars — Mick Ronson, Trevor Bolder and Mick Woodmansey. Producing the album was Ken Scott. He had previously worked as an engineer on Bowie's 1970 album, *The Man Who Sold The World*, as well as with the Beatles. Also involved with the sessions was Rick Wakeman on piano. Upon

Why The Rise And Fall Of Ziggy Stardust?

completion of the sessions, Wakeman declined Bowie's invite to be a member of The Spiders (a pivotal decision considering that not long after, Wakeman would go on to join the iconic progressive rock band, Yes).

The sessions for both *Hunky Dory* and *Ziggy Stardust* were incredibly close together. Just as well really considering that it was mutually agreed that the majority of songs on *Hunky Dory* were not sufficient material with which to go on tour.

Hunky Dory was released in December 1971 and the 'Changes' single came out in January 1972. Despite managing to get radio airplay, the single didn't chart in the UK that time around. Although *Hunky Dory* was given a positive welcome by the critics, it didn't do well commercially. That too failed to chart in the UK.

New Musical Express advocated; "A breath of fresh air compared to the usual mainstream rock LP of today. It's very possible that this will be the most important album from an emerging artist in 1972, because he's not following trends — he's setting them… *Hunky Dory* is a masterpiece from a mastermind."

Melody Maker enthused: "Not only the best album Bowie has ever done, it's also the most inventive piece of songwriting to have appeared on record for a considerable period of time."

Rolling Stone asserted; "*Hunky Dory* not only represents Bowie's most engaging album musically, but also finds him once more writing literally enough to let the listener examine his ideas comfortably... With his affection for using intriguing and unusual themes in musical settings that most rock "artists" would dismiss with a quick fart as old-fashioned and uncool, he's definitely an original, is David Bowie, and as such will one day make an album that will induce us homo superior elitist rock critics to race about like a chicken with its head lopped off when he learns that he's a couple of pretentious tendencies he'd do handsomely to curtail through the composition of an album's-worth of material. Until that time, *Hunky Dory* will suffice hunky-dorily."

Melody Maker considered in February 1972; "Bowie, who has hardly performed in public since his 'Space Oddity' hit of three years ago, is coming back in super-style. In the States, critics have hailed him as the new Bob Dylan, and his tour de force album *Hunky Dory* looks set to enter the British charts. 'Changes', the single taken from it, was Tony Blackburn's Record Of The Week recently."

It was anticipated by some that *Hunky Dory* would do for Bowie what *The Man Who Sold The World* hadn't. *Melody Maker* advocated in the same feature; "They call David a lot of things. In the States he's been referred to as the English Bob Dylan and an avant-garde outrage, all rolled up together. *The New York Times* talks of his 'coherent and brilliant vision'. They like him a lot there. Back home in the very stiff upper lip UK, where people are outraged by Alice Cooper even, there ain't too many who have picked up on him. His last but one album *The Man Who Sold The World*, cleared 50,000 copies in the States; here it sold about five copies, and Bowie bought them. Yes, but before this year is out all those of you who puked up on Alice are going to be focusing your passions on Mr Bowie, and those who know where it's at will be thrilling to a voice that seemingly undergoes brilliant metamorphosis from song to song, a songwriting ability that will enslave the heart, and a sense of theatrics that will make the ablest thespians gnaw on their sticks of eyeliner in envy. All this and an amazingly accomplished band, featuring super-lead guitarist Mick Ronson, that can smack you round the skull with their heaviness and soothe the savage beasts with their delicacy. Oh, to be young again. The reason is Bowie's new album *Hunky Dory*, which combines a gift for irresistible melody lines with lyrics that work on several levels — as straight forward narrative, philosophy or allegory, depending how deep you wish to plumb the depths.

He has a knack of suffusing strong, simple pop melodies with words and arrangements full of mystery and darkling hints."

Although things were looking up overall, RCA didn't quite know how best to promote Bowie. Fortunately though, his image was about to change and with that, so were the opportunities for promotion.

Despite having a musically strong discography prior to the release of *Ziggy Stardust*, commercially, it hadn't always been plain sailing for Bowie. With the advantage of hindsight, it is easy to look back on Bowie's career and assume that it had been commercially sparkling from the beginning. Prior to 1972 in particular though, this hadn't always been the case.

In fact, from entering the charts in late 1969, Bowie was soon out of them again — a virtual disappearance from the pop world. The re-emergence in 1972 presented some of the most controversial sights and sounds ever witnessed in an industry which has always thrived on the controversial. By the end of '72 he was a superstar: one of the rare ones who did it on the strength of his stage persona as well as his recorded talent. Journalists didn't ask David Bowie what his favourite food was, or his favourite colour, or his personal preference in night attire, or any of the banal questions that were normally fired at upcoming pop stars.

Take Paul McCartney for instance. When the Beatles first hit the bemused eardrums of a fan-following brought up on a diet of boy-next-door-type lyrics, Paul was prepared to go along with the questioning. It transpired that he was exceptionally fond of Kraft cheese slices, black socks, and jelly babies. He soon wished he hadn't been quite so flippant. After all, there is a limit to how many cheese slices one can eat, and for sure you can only wear, at best, two pairs of black socks at the same time. As for jelly babies, well, if flung with sufficient power at a musician partly blinded by the spotlights, ouch!

David Bowie, superstar, hadn't developed in that kind

of scene. He was carefully managed in his big-star days, and protected from the overexposure that so often hit the pop giants. Excessive coverage of a star could turn the public off where before they were turned on. So, prior to 1972, the Bowie story was *not* studded with facts and figures about his personal life. There was plenty to be said about his influence on the pop scene though. He so often behaved like a musical chameleon at the start of his career that his story up to that point was inevitably one of fits and starts, hops and jumps. It is therefore vital to consider what pop music was like when he first jumped into the charts.

In September '69, 'Space Oddity' peaked at number five in the UK. Backed by 'Wild Eyed Boy From Freecloud' on the B-side, it was Bowie's first single for the Philips group, coming out on Mercury. He said at the time that it was the first single he was keen to release. He wrote both sides, and co-arranged them with Paul Buckmaster, one of the world's finest arrangers of pop-type string sections. Recorded at London's Trident Studios, the single was produced by Gus Dudgeon and engineered by one Barry Sheffield. A stellar cast list, they contributed their talents to create what was one of the finest singles of that year.

It could be said that 1969 was an unusual year for pop music; whilst many were bemoaning a lack of activity from the Beatles – who'd dominated the scene since 1962 – they were left wondering who, or what, was going to emerge to trigger off a new excitement. As a result, the pop world into which 'Space Oddity' was launched was going round in circles, rather than launching into a new orbit. Top artists of the previous year had been a pretty mixed bunch. Fleetwood Mac were big, perhaps a little more so than the arguing and declining Beatles. Solo stars performing best in the charts were Stevie Wonder, Marvin Gaye, Elvis Presley, Frank Sinatra, The Hollies and the Bee Gees. Frankly, not a lot was new. Peter Sarstedt had topped the charts with a beautiful song called 'Where Do You Go To (My

Lovely)?', but he couldn't find the flair or the sound to follow it up. There was the odd outbreak of reggae, via Desmond Dekker and Johnny Nash and the like. Amen Corner, The Move, The Foundations, The Archies — all with hit records, but just ponder where they were three years thereafter.

In late 1969, David presented his album, *David Bowie*. It was such an eye-opener. So many people had become aware of him through 'Space Oddity' but here, before their ears, was a set of first-rate, neatly styled songs. The album featured members of the band Junior's Eyes helping out substantially on the backings, along with session musicians Rick Wakeman, Herbie Flowers and Paul Buckmaster. Though the general pattern was for a big hit single to be followed by a big hit album, there were no sensational sales of Bowie's excellent LP. It did well enough. But what followed it was a long spell where his involvement in the music business – in terms of acting the recording idol – was minimal. He was busy putting his ideas and theories together; he was to have a long spell of hibernation before anything new would appear.

In terms of the scope to be recognised as a hit-maker in the pop popularity polls of 1969, Bowie was a bit late to the party. Still though, in a few of them he was listed along with the likes of balladeer Malcolm Roberts, bassist Jack Bruce, guitarist Peter Green, Jethro Tull frontman Ian Anderson and so on. In one poll, he even beat Led Zeppelin's Robert Plant, and indeed Joe Cocker. 1969 and 'Space Oddity' certainly wasn't a terrible start for Bowie, it's just that it wasn't a flying one either.

No matter what was to come, Bowie's groundwork in pop music had guaranteed that he would be accepted as a worthwhile talent and not just as a fly-by-night character with good teeth, a photogenic smile and a good head of hair. He had been doing things the right way round: laying the foundation before building on a career as a pop hit-maker.

Essentially, it's easy to look back on the careers of many

artists who were big in the seventies and make the assumption that from the late sixties onwards, their success was going to be inevitable. Really though, upon closer examination, it becomes clear that with the emergence of a new decade and with Beatlemania being very much on the decline, there was very much a feeling amongst the entire music industry of "what now?" and "sure, artists are still making good music, but what does the public want? And how do we promote this accordingly?" In terms of the late sixties and very early seventies, it could certainly be argued that Bowie was one of many who was perhaps at risk of slipping through the net.

There is no disputing Bowie's talent, but certainly in the early days, it could be said that good management certainly went in his favour. From the sixties onwards, many artists aspired to make it big in America. Along with his manager, Tony Defries, by late 1971 David Bowie was clearly ambitious. Consequently, it had seen them take a trip to New York in hopes of raising Bowie's profile. The trip was made with the intention of securing a record deal. Such was the sense of ambition that a very deliberate decision had been made to stay at the luxury Warwick Hotel. Famously, the Beatles had stayed there previously. Defries masterfully manufactured a situation that would get Bowie seen by all the right people.

The deal made with RCA was worth $37,000 which, at the time, was a modest amount of money for the industry. Defries wasn't worried though; he knew that it was a good starting point and that the only way was up. With the contract having been signed on 9th September 1971, this certainly proved to be true. When Defries had terminated Bowie's contract with Mercury Records, RCA hadn't been the only label that he had tried appealing to but RCA was certainly a good match. Bowie would remain on the label for the rest of the seventies.

During the days that followed the trip to New York, Bowie set to work preparing for what would be an unofficial debut with the yet-to-be-named Spiders From Mars. Aylesbury Friars was the venue of choice for them. Just outside of London, it was known for its welcoming audiences. The former Animals pianist Tom Parker was invited to play this gig on account of the fact that Rick Wakeman had started with Yes just a few weeks earlier. Taking to the stage at Friars on 25th September 1971, Bowie was apparently anxious. Nevertheless, the performance marked the start of something big.

On 28th April 1972 — just over a month before the *Ziggy Stardust* album was released — the public were given a hint of what to expect with the release of 'Starman'. Recorded at a separate session at Trident Studios after the majority of songs had already been recorded for the album, 'Starman' was a last-minute replacement for the track 'Round And Round' (which was omitted from the album altogether). The recording of 'Starman' took place after it had been decided that a song was needed to function as a main single to promote the album. It was on 4th February 1972 at Trident that the track was completed. 'Starman' proved to be an excellent choice; it got to number ten in the UK charts. In the US though, it only got to number sixty-five.

Bowie said in an interview with an American radio station in February 1972; "'Round And Round' would have been the perfect kind of number that Ziggy would have done on stage. I think probably what happened, is that it was a jam. We jammed 'Round And Round' for old time's sake in the studio and the enthusiasm of the jam probably waned after we heard the track a few times and we replaced it with a thing called 'Starman'."

When the *Ziggy Stardust* album was released in June 1972, BBC Radio broadcast a version of 'Starman' that had been recorded in one of its studios on 22nd May exclusively for promotional purposes. This version was broadcast by the BBC a total of four times on Johnnie Walker's radio show up to and including 9th June.

David Bowie - *The Rise And Fall Of Ziggy Stardust*

When David and The Spiders filmed their performance of 'Starman' for *Top Of The Pops* on 5th July 1972 (to be broadcast on the 6th), the single was only at number forty one. Robin Lumley joined them on keyboards (two years later Lumley would go on to be a founding member of the jazz rock band Brand X, which also featured Genesis' Phil Collins). A backing tape was used for the song but guitar and vocals were performed live. Bowie's costume and hairstyle added a uniqueness to his performance, as did the way in which he sung the song with his arm around Mick Ronson. Although this TV performance of 'Starman' is perhaps the most memorable one from this period, prior to going on *Top Of The Pops*, Bowie and The Spiders had also performed it on 15th June on *Lift Off With Ayeshea* (a popular children's show broadcast in the afternoon).

John Peel reviewed 'Starman' for *Disc* in April 1972; "Now this is magnificent — quite superb. We played this fifteen times, roaring along with the lyrics and boogying in front of the fire. When I'd finished listening to all the other records, we played it a few times more. David Bowie is, with Kevin Ayers, the most important, under-acknowledged innovator in contemporary popular music in Britain and if this record is overlooked it will be nothing less than stark tragedy. It's four minutes and ten seconds of major achievement. It starts slow, brooding, menacing, with little hint of the massive power and exaltation to come."

"David mumbles one or two indistinct lines behind the instrumentation before starting on the song proper. 'Starman' is out there in the sky waiting and 'he'd like to come and meet us but he's afraid he'd blow our minds.' Sometimes the lyrics are hard to catch but the story seems to be that Starman takes over radio from his waiting station in space — 'that were no D.J., that was Hazy Cosmic Jive'. Then he's on TV as well but 'don't tell your Papa, he'll get us locked up'. 'Let The Children Boogie' he seems to say and there follows a thudding, hand-clapping, body-shaking slow boogie that must be Mick Ronson and Mick Woodmansey. Jesus — it feels good. The whole record is a sheer orgiastic delight. If you hear it a few times you're never going to be able to ignore it. A classic, a gem — what more can I say to convince you? The B-side is David in Velvet Underground mood and it's a shuddering, slightly malevolent stomper. 'That's great, is that B-side' said Pig from the other room — and it is good enough to be an A-side at that. Good on yer."

The single was reviewed by *New Musical Express* in the same month; "David proves he's not just a pretty face on this cosmic forty-five. This is quite an elevating and energetic song with some super "teenage" lyrics. It takes a few listens to do it to ya, but 'Starman' is obviously single of the week. The B-side — 'Suffragette City' is one of the many highlights of David's monumental live performances."

And *Melody Maker*; "'There's a Starman waiting in the sky' says David in that strange voice filled with premonitions and doom. 'He'd like to meet us but he's afraid he'd blow our minds.' Fascinating lyrics as usual and a space truckin' tune that should appeal to all at Mission Control and points west. David is taking longer than most to become a superstar, but he should catch up with Rod and Marc soon. There was a lot of talent wandering loose in the mid-sixties. Whose left from those days who hasn't made it yet? George Catsmeat! — of course!"

And *Record Mirror*; "May take a bit of time to register at full power, but this sounds a definite hit for the talented David. Good, strong guitar backing, a rather rambling opening, but later on he sings out with both personality and dramatics. He is a first-class performer, this bloke and that is herewith translated to disc."

And *Sounds*; "Bowie has been around a long time waiting in the wings to pick up on the echelons of glory that have come to many of his contemporaries. In an effort to come through with impact he has developed his outward appearance into a succession of "high camp" poses. Certainly it's brought the press scurrying but I don't know whether it's strengthened his position as an artist in this country. Which, in a way, is a shame because — and I hasten to say this — his talents as musician and writer are unchanged from their former brilliance and have, if anything, come through strengthened in the past year or so. 'Starman' is, as nearly all his tracks these days, a perfect example of David's very underrated talents. In many ways it's atmospherically comparable to 'Space Oddity' with the Mellotron and guitar work that came to light on that lauded track. It doesn't have quite the same instant appeal about it until the chorus line takes off — which unfortunately may be a little too late to get it into the chart. But it's well worth having: 'Let all the children boogie' and I like the 'Reach Out' rip off midway through."

Chapter Two
The Making Of

In an interview for an American radio station in February 1972, when asked if he could explain a bit about his upcoming album, Bowie said; "I'll try very hard. It's a little difficult but it originally started as a concept album, but it kind of got broken up because I found other songs I wanted to put in the album which wouldn't have fitted into the story of Ziggy — so at the moment it's a little fractured and a little fragmented. Anyway, what you have there on that album when it does finally come out is a story which doesn't really take place — it's just a few little scenes from the life of a band called Ziggy Stardust and The Spiders From Mars, who could feasibly be the last band on Earth — it could be within the last five years of Earth. I'm not at all sure, because I wrote it in such a way that I just dropped the numbers into the album in any order that they cropped up. It depends in which state you listen to it in. The times that I've listened to it — I've had a number of meanings out of the album, but I always do. Once I've written an album, my interpretations of the numbers in that album are totally different afterwards than the time that I wrote them and I find that I learn a lot from my own albums about me."

He told *New Musical Express* in July 1972; "One can say a sentence to three people and it'll take on an entirely different meaning for each of those three people. I think if any of my stuff becomes at all surrealistic it's because that's the purpose of it. It's to give people their own definitions. I certainly don't understand half the stuff I write. I can look back on a song that

I have just written and it means something entirely different now because of my new circumstances, new this or that. I get told by so many people — especially Americans — what my songs are about."

The Songs

'Five Years' was recorded in November 1971 at Trident Studios. The song was first played to the public on 7th February 1972 on the BBC radio show, *Sounds Of The Seventies*. The following day, Bowie's performance of the song (along with 'Queen Bitch' and 'Oh! You Pretty Things') featured on *The Old Grey Whistle Test*. Excellent promotion considering that the *Ziggy Stardust* album would not be released for another four months. The song depicts the story of the Earth's impending doom. Disaster is just around the corner and soon mankind will be obliterated. So why was five years the choice of time period? Why did Bowie say that there were five years until doomsday? Well, in 1972 he simply told a journalist that he made his choice because "it was a bad afternoon."

More profoundly, Bowie said in 1973; "It has been announced that the world will end because of lack of natural resources. Ziggy is in a position where all the kids have access to things that they thought they wanted. The older people have lost all touch with reality and the kids are left on their own to plunder anything. Ziggy was in a rock 'n' roll band and the kids no longer want rock 'n' roll. There's no electricity to play it. Ziggy's advisors tell him to collect news and sing it, because there is no news. So Ziggy does this and there is terrible news."

Bowie was asked about the lyric, "I never knew I'd need so many people." He was quoted in *New Musical Express* in July 1972; "Basically what it means is realising the inevitability of the apocalypse, in whatever form it takes. I was being careful not to say what form it would take because that to me would be incredibly sad and I just tried to get that feeling over in one line. It's like the things you flash on supposedly when you're dying running down the street and... the grasping for life."

Bowie recorded the vocal part for 'Five Years' in just two takes. The two takes were done for technical reasons in terms of how Bowie's vocals at the beginning of the song start off quietly. In contrast of course, his voice gets much louder further into the song and so consequently, it was necessary to do two takes in order that the levels could be adjusted appropriately in production. Ronson's guitar parts that occur at the end of the song were done in just one take.

Technical expertise aside, the song was performed with emotion in the studio. So much so that Bowie was crying by the end of doing it. Just the four words, "we've got five years", had to be redone a few times on account of how Bowie's emotional performance made them incomprehensible the first few times around.

As the opening track on the album, 'Five Years' sets the mood in terms of how the drum beat that introduces the song sets a strong sense of atmosphere. The intense apocalyptic theme of the song is such that a lot of thought went into choosing the exact drum beat to use — not just the rhythm but the actual drums.

The way in which the song fades in and fades out again was also a deliberate decision in terms of what Bowie wanted to convey thematically — the idea of something coming from nothing and going to nothing.

Throughout the whole track, the drum part had no effect added to it in production. However, a reverb is present where the sound of the orchestra dies out.

The beat for the second song on the album, 'Soul Love', comes in as 'Five Years' fades out. The song is about the different kinds of love. Stone Love is love for the departed, New Love is romantic love and Soul Love is a religious love. Overall, the song is a love song but less typical in its exploration of the subject. Of course, whilst Bowie himself didn't explicitly explain his intentions behind the song, the general interpretation among many is that it's not merely about a romantic and/or sexual love in a boy-meets-girl kind of way.

Across the whole Ziggy Stardust tour period, 'Soul Love' was only performed live on the second US leg.

'Moonage Daydream' is the third song. It introduces the character of Ziggy Stardust. It is the first electric guitar based song on the album — Mick Ronson plays a Les Paul.

With the exception of the first tour of the UK, the song was performed live at all of the 1972 and 1973 Ziggy Stardust concerts. In some instances, Bowie introduced it as "a song written by Ziggy". He was quoted in *Rolling Stone* in January 1976; "My friend came to mind, standing the way we stood in 'Bewlay Brothers' and I wrote 'Moonage Daydream'."

An early version of the song had been recorded in April 1971 at Radio Luxemburg's London Studios — intended as the first single for Bowie's Arnold Corns project. This version features a different arrangement as well as different lyrics. The re-recorded version of 'Moonage Daydream' is that which features on the *Ziggy Stardust* album. This version was recorded at Trident Studios in November 1971. A special recording of this version was broadcast on *Top Gear* on 25th July 1972.

In subsequent years Ken Scott, Trevor Bolder and Woody Woodmansey all said that they consider 'Moonage Daydream' as one of their favourites from the *Ziggy Stardust* album.

The song is a futuristic rock and roll number. When Bowie introduced it to the Spiders, Woodmansey in particular felt that it was very different to anything that Bowie had written before. As a result, a lot of thought was put into how they could best approach the song in a way that would ensure it would fit in with the other ones that they were working on at time. Woodmansey's first impression of the song was that it sounded rather folk-like; the challenge was in how to break it down into something that would fit the format of rock and roll. It was an important task considering that 'Moonage Daydream' ultimately ended up becoming so lyrically and thematically central to the album overall.

Mick Ronson contributed his solo in layers, consequently making for a very space-like sound. Despite the more experimental aspects of the song, the entire band kept a solid beat going. The end result is a unique and iconic track.

When telling Ken Scott about the sound he was aiming for, Bowie was precise. In later years Bowie told of how his use of the pennywhistle and baritone sax came about: "The solo in it is a baritone sax and it was supposed to have been a fife but we couldn't find anyone who played fife so I ended up playing penny whistle — so it's baritone sax and penny whistle and I got that combination of instruments from the B-side of The Hollywood Argyle's 'Alley Oop'. On the other side was the song 'Sho Know A Lot About Love'. And the solo of that was fife and baritone sax and I thought that's the greatest combination of instruments. It's so ludicrous — you've got this tiny sparrow of a voice on top and a huge grunting pig ox of a thing at the bottom."

Apparently, the swirling string part that occurs at the end of 'Moonage Daydream' was added by Ken Scott later on in the mixing process. A lot of reverb was added to the higher notes, but not so much the lower notes.

The fifth track, 'Starman', was made in response to how it was felt that the album lacked a song that would be suitable for a single.

Prior to the recording of 'Starman', when material for *Ziggy Stardust* was presented to RCA, the general consensus was that a single needed to be made. History has it of course, that commercially, 'Starman' did wonders for Bowie but at the time there were still concerns that it could be *too* commercial. Sure, Bowie and The Spiders had been asked to make a song that would be suitable for single release but in doing so, it was new territory for them. One of the amazing things about 'Starman' though, is that upon being asked to write something that could be a single, Bowie didn't write a series of songs and then narrow it down via process of elimination; he simply wrote 'Starman' and that was it. In later years, Woodmansey advocated that Bowie was good at fulfilling the brief and had he wanted to, he could have probably written many more commercial singles throughout his career.

'Starman' was the first of Bowie's songs to have commercial appeal after his 1969 single, 'Space Oddity'. Not only was 'Starman' vital to the success of *Ziggy Stardust*; it put the idea of a concept across. This was very much the case visually as well when the song was performed on *Top Of The Pops*. In a fascinating coincidence of contrasts, when Bowie and The Spiders were waiting to do their performance for the show, they were stood in the corridor next to Status Quo who of course, were clad in their trademark denim! Rumour has it that Francis Rossi said to them, "Shit, you make us feel old."

The US release of the 'Starman' single is a slightly different edit of the song to what features on the UK version. The US version has at least ten seconds less of the song's fadeout. Some sources state that it was Dennis Katz at RCA who was adamant that 'Starman' needed to be included on *Ziggy Stardust*.

Around the time of the release of *Ziggy Stardust*, Bowie had mentioned the possibility of an album to bridge the gap between the latter and *Hunky Dory*. The album that never came to be was going to include the following songs: 'Starman', 'Bombers', 'He's A Goldmine', 'Something Happens' and 'Round And Round'. All five songs had been considered for the

Ziggy Stardust album, but of course, only 'Starman' made the final cut. Contrastingly, Ken Scott insists that no such project was ever in the works.

'Starman' conveys the story of a extraterrestrial being trying to get in touch with the young people of Earth via the radio in an effort to offer them salvation. In doing this, the extraterrestrial is anxious about the effect his intervention could have. Bowie said of the song in 1972; "'Starman' can be taken at the immediate level of 'There's a Starman in the sky saying boogie children', but the theme of it is that the idea of things in the sky is really quite human and real and we should be a bit happier about the prospect of meeting people." And in 1974; "'Starman' was the song that Ziggy wrote which inspired people to follow him and it was all a pack of lies but he continued and then he was crushed by his own ego."

Overall, 'Starman' is an uplifting song. And of course, it wasn't Bowie's first exploration into the theme of space.

According to the lore that Bowie created with the view to doing a Ziggy Stardust musical (which sadly never happened), a community of "starmen" tell the human Ziggy Stardust to write about their impending visit to Earth. In writing 'Starman', Ziggy is first able to get the message across that the Earth will be no more in five years' time.

On the cassette release of *Ziggy Stardust*, 'Starman' is at the start of side two having swapped places with 'Lady Stardust'.

The last song on side one of the LP is 'It Ain't Easy'. Recorded on the 9th September at Trident Studios, it was originally considered for inclusion on *Hunky Dory*. Consequently, it was the first song to be recorded that made it onto the *Ziggy Stardust* album.

'It Ain't Easy' is the only song on *Ziggy Stardust* not to have been written by Bowie. It was written by Ron Davies. The American penned song had been covered by many artists in the early seventies including Three Dog Night in 1970 and Long John Baldry in 1971. Dave Edmunds did a version of the song for his 1971 *Rockpile* album.

Bowie didn't perform 'It Ain't Easy' live — not on the Ziggy Stardust tour and not thereafter. He did however, do a live recording of it for John Peel's *Sunday Concert* on 5th June 1971.

To some, 'It Ain't Easy' doesn't match the overall feel of the *Ziggy Stardust* album, especially in view of the fact that there was such a wealth of other material that could have been used. On balance though, even before the album was released, Bowie seemed unapologetic about all of the songs made that weren't chosen for the final cut. He said in an interview for American radio in February 1972; "I've kept them all. I think that maybe we could put them out as a budget album or something at a later date, the stuff that never really got used. Because there are quite a few."

On the original release of *Ziggy Stardust*, Dana Gillespie wasn't credited for her backing vocals and neither was Rick Wakeman for his contribution on harpsichord. This has been rectified on recent reissues of the album.

'Lady Stardust' is the first song of side two. Bowie said of the song in later years, "This, I think, is a really lovely song. It sounds really good even today. I like this one — I think it's a good bit of songwriting." Working titles for the song were 'He Was Alright (The Band Was Altogether)', 'A Song For Marc' and 'He Was Alright (A Song For Marc)' (a demo of it had been recorded in April 1971).

On 19th June 1972, a special recording of 'Lady Stardust' was broadcast on *Sounds Of The Seventies*.

The second track on side two, 'Star', was recorded in November 1971 at Trident Studios. The song was originally going to be called 'Rock 'n' Roll Star'.

Before it had been decided that 'Star' would be included on *Ziggy Stardust*, in early 1971 Bowie had offered the song to a little known UK band by the name of Chameleon (their lead singer was Les Payne). A demo tape of 'Star' had been recorded at Radio Luxemburg Studios and had been sent to Payne for consideration. Payne had wanted Bowie to produce the song for them but with Chameleon being under the Chrysalis label, they had been told that they could only do the song with a "proper" producer. Ouch! Consequently, the song was given back to Bowie.

The demo in question was auctioned at Christie's Auction House in Kensington in September 2000. It sold for £1,527. Existing on a half inch reel-to-reel studio tape, the demo recording is apparently considerably different to the version that came to be made for *Ziggy Stardust*. It is reported that the opening lines to the song 'Tony went to fight in Belfast, Rudi stayed at home to starve' were originally written as 'If someone had the sense to hear me, if someone had the time to see'. And that the chorus lyrics of 'I could make it all worthwhile as a rock 'n' roll star' and 'I could make a transformation as a rock 'n' roll star' were originally written as 'I could make a big time noise as a rock 'n' roll star'.

Bowie said that he borrowed the backing vocal line in 'Star' from the Beatles' song, 'Lovely Rita'.

The third song on side two, 'Hang On To Yourself', was performed at all of the Ziggy Stardust shows. It was often used as the opening number. In later years Mick Ronson joked of his role in the song, "Strap the guitar on, and thrash it to death, basically." The song was originally recorded at Radio Luxemburg Studios in 1971 as part of the Arnold Corns project.

Special recordings of 'Hang On To Yourself' were broadcast on *Sounds Of The Seventies* on 28th January 1972 and again on the same programme on 7th February, as well as on *Top Gear* on 23rd May 1972.

For the recording of 'Hang On To Yourself' that appears on *Ziggy Stardust*, Ken Scott was keen to punctuate the song with Bowie's acoustic guitar — more so than honing in on the cymbals.

'Ziggy Stardust' is a vital track; it explains the rise and fall of the character and is thus essential to the album. It was recorded in the November 1971 sessions. Special recordings of the song were broadcast on *Sounds Of The Seventies* on 28th January and 7th February 1972, as well as on *Top Gear* on 23rd May. The song was performed as part of every gig on the Ziggy Stardust tour.

Not only is 'Ziggy Stardust' important in terms of how it conveys a vital theme on the album, it also showcases Mick Ronson's unique and excellent guitar sound. He played his Les Paul through a Marshall amp but a lot was achieved through his use of a pedal — a Cry Baby wah-wah.

In terms of the futuristic feel of the song, in later years Woodmansey told of how at the time, he was strongly influenced by King Crimson whereby drum rolls occurred in unusual places in a song.

The penultimate song, 'Suffragette City' was recorded at Trident Studios sometime between 12th and 18th January 1972. Special recordings of the song were broadcast on *Top Gear* on 23rd May and 25th July 1972. The song was performed as part of every gig on the Ziggy Stardust tour.

A demo of 'Suffragette City' had first been offered to Mott The Hoople in 1971. Bowie had wanted to help them out as the band was suffering financial difficulty at the time.

Although it sounds like there is a saxophone on 'Suffragette City', the sound was in fact made by an ARP 2500 synthesiser.

The Making Of

The sound that Bowie wanted to create on the track was bigger than anything that he could play himself and so consequently, the synthesiser was the instrument of choice in this instance.

As the last song on *Ziggy Stardust*, 'Rock 'n' Roll Suicide', like 'Suffragette City', was recorded sometime between 12th and 18th January 1972 at Trident Studios. A special recording of the song was broadcast on *Sounds Of The Seventies* on 19th June 1972. Performed at all of the Ziggy Stardust performances, 'Rock 'n' Roll Suicide' was typically done as the last number.

At the time of writing 'Rock 'n' Roll Suicide', Bowie held the belief that a famous rock star would soon be killed on stage. He feared that it would be him. He said of the song in later years though; "At this point I had a passion for the idea of a rock star as a meteor and the whole idea of The Who's line "hope I die before I get old". At that youthful age you cannot believe that you'll lose the ability to be this enthusiastic and all-knowing about the world, life and experience. You think you've probably discovered all the secrets to life. 'Rock 'n' Roll Suicide' was a declaration of the end of the effect of being young."

Of the lyrics, "time takes a cigarette..." Bowie later admitted; "That was a sort of plagiarised line from Baudelaire which was something to the effect of 'life is a cigarette, smoke it in a hurry or savour it'."

In recording the song, the levels were set to allow for Bowie to sing quietly and close to the microphone. An emotional song, it's no coincidence that 'Rock 'n' Roll Suicide' was chosen to be the final song on *Ziggy Stardust*.

Album Artwork

The album's cover features Bowie dressed in a jumpsuit on a quiet backstreet. He looks like an outsider. It was a deliberate decision in terms of the theme of the album.

The photos that feature on the front and back of *Ziggy Stardust* were taken on 13th January 1972 by Brian Ward. A total of fifty-four photos were taken on the shoot on Heddon Street — the location of Ward's studio. Prior to the shoot, Bowie had phoned Ward and made the request for a location that looked like a Brooklyn alley scene.

Bowie said of the photoshoot; "It was cold and it rained and I felt like an actor. We did the photographs outside on a rainy night... upstairs in the studio we did the *Clockwork Orange* look-a-likes that became the inner album sleeve."

The photos of Bowie and The Spiders that feature on the inner sleeve of the album were designed to have a very *Clockwork Orange* feel to them; it is no coincidence. Bowie told *Rolling Stone* in 1993; "The idea was to hit a look somewhere between the Malcolm McDowell thing with the one mascaraed eyelash and insects. It was the era of *Wild Boys* by William S. Burroughs. That was a really heavy book that had come out in about 1970, and it was a cross between that and *Clockwork Orange* that really started to put together the shape and the look of what Ziggy and The Spiders were going to become. They were both powerful pieces of work, especially the marauding boy gangs of Burrough's *Wild Boys* with their Bowie knives. I got straight on to that. I read everything into everything. Everything had to be infinitely symbolic."

The initial photos were shot in black and white. They were then colourised by Terry Pastor of Main Artery. Although Bowie's jumpsuit was colourised to be turquoise, it was in fact the same grey/green one that he wore for his performance on *The Old Grey Whistle Test* in February 1972. Also, Bowie's hair was a mousey blond colour when the photos were taken but the images were colourised to give him a bold yellow hair colour.

The K. West sign in the cover photo was the name of a furrier company that operated from the nearby building. The company no longer exists.

Although the phone box was replaced in the 1980s by a smaller model and then eventually, others, the walls surrounding it continue to be decorated with messages that pay homage to Bowie and Ziggy Stardust.

Release and Reviews

The Rise And Fall Of Ziggy Stardust And The Spiders From Mars was released in June 1972. It remained in the US chart for over a year, despite the fact that it only peaked at number seventy-five there.

Record Mirror reviewed the album in June 1972; "There's no denying that David Bowie is totally individual. A Bowie-album is like no other, and all his offerings so far have been entertaining. Though I find the opening track the weakest as far as the vocal is concerned, the subject is handled cleverly, giving a new dimension to the revelation that the world has only five years more to go. 'Soul Love' is a total piece of brilliance with far away vocal phrases, an insistent drum rhythm and smooth Bowie sax — it would make a strong single, though the chosen track 'Starman' should have been gobbled up by the public. 'It Ain't Easy' — the lyrics are missing from the inner sleeve for some reason — is a big vocal builder, with a nice guitar and piano ending."

In the same month, *New Musical Express* considered; "With most of his material either dealing with the flashier style of city living or looking far into the future, Bowie must rate as our most futuristic songwriter. Sometimes what he sees is just a little scary, and perhaps there's a bit more pessimism here than on previous releases, but they're still fine songs. Like the first track, 'Five Years', about the imminent death of a decaying world, is a real downer to start with, but Bowie brings a new approach to the rather overworked theme."

"Certainly all the tracks – written by Bowie with the exception of Ron Davies' 'It Ain't Easy' – are never less than entertaining. 'Soul Love' features some withdrawn sax. 'Ziggy Stardust' deals with the destruction of a rock star, while 'Hang On To Yourself' is a real little sexual gem. Also included is Bowie's current single 'Starman'. Mick Ronson (guitar), Trevor Bolder (bass) and Mick Woodmansey (drums) handle the backing all through. Of course there's nothing Bowie would like more than to be a glittery superstar, and it could still come to pass. By now everybody ought to know he's tremendous and this latest chunk of fantasy can only enhance his reputation further. Mick Ronson's piano work also dominates the opener to side two, 'Lady Stardust', with Bowie providing some excellent vocals, with a harmony line that reminds me in some obscure way of Beatle harmonies. There's some up-tempo rock styled material here, like in the whirling 'Hang On To Yourself' and the lovely line 'but then we move around like tigers on Vaseline' which for me sums up totally the mastery that Bowie has with words. There's also mellower moments, and the overall production is excellent. People, listen."

Circus reviewed it in July 1972; "Someday in the far future when armed guides are leading interplanetary tourists through the ruins of Western society, perhaps they'll also be touting chrome statuettes of David Bowie — the young man from England who, if it may not be said that he saw it coming, at least was heard to cry 'Look out!' David's latest exclamation comes in the form of this portrait-in-song of the ultimate rock and roll star. Ziggy is an otherworldly figure who can really sing and 'lick 'em by smiling'. With the lyrical expertise he

The Making Of

has demonstrated in *Hunky Dory* and earlier albums, Bowie dispassionately chronicles Ziggy's upward course, his reign at the top, and his inevitable decline. From start to finish this is an LP of dazzling intensity and mad design. Bowie is achieving with words the sort of effect which groups like Pink Floyd are attempting with instruments and volume. At times one is almost mesmerised by the tumble of images and the sheer force of Bowie's performance. A stunning work of genius. Not your everyday sort of album, but an album for every day — at least until the end."

From *Oz Magazine* the same month: "David Bowie, easily the most brilliant young songwriter in this country, seems to have been going through quite a few rapid changes over the last year or so. It all started with the release of his miserably underrated *Man Who Sold The World*, which portrayed him as some bisexual Greta Garbo figure with rather tortured Nietzsche overtones! The neurotic elements of that album manifested themselves in part of the schizophrenic *Hunky Dory*, but now things have developed even further. *The Rise And Fall Of Ziggy Stardust* personifies Bowie's new image as the intended messiah of Teenage Wasteland. Live, he is an almost grotesque parody of early Elvis Presley complete with outrageously tasteless costume, butch hairstyle and calculated effeminate gestures."

"On the new album, Bowie attempts to live and fully verbalise his fantasies. *Ziggy Stardust* is his wish fulfilment — 'came on so loaded man... well hung and snow white tan' — the last great superstar before the apocalypse (fully described in the first track 'Five Years'), who is eventually torn to pieces by his fans in a scene straight out of Nik Cohn's *I Am Still The Greatest, Says Johnny Angelo*. The only problem is that it all doesn't quite come off and this all becomes very clear once one has witnessed his awkward posturings on stage. Bowie is over-reaching himself, trying to cover too much ground. The

David Bowie - *The Rise And Fall Of Ziggy Stardust*

character he ultimately portrays has more in common with the amazing Iggy Stooge than anything Bowie could extend himself to. All of which is sad because taken on its own terms, the *Ziggy Stardust* album is quite superb."

"Bowie is now working in new areas, having been studying the art of punk rock poetry from Lou Reed, while effectively developing his own talents in the realm of his lyrical fascination for science fiction. His unique sexual imagery (previously best illustrated in *The Man Who Sold The World*'s chilling 'She Shook Me Cold') has lost its neurotic edge, giving way to lines like 'This mellow-thighed chick just put my spine out of place' or, even better, 'we move around like tigers on Vaseline'. The best track of all is the single 'Starman' which is perfect pulp sci-fi rock complete with killer chorus. *The Rise And Fall Of Ziggy Stardust And The Spiders From Mars* is the vital link around which Bowie's new image is to be projected, and I have a feeling it will, if only temporarily, succeed. It's all a little unfortunate, though, that someone as capable as David Bowie should attempt to hype himself as something he isn't."

And from *Records & Recording*: "There are rock albums and there are rock albums. This is one of the latter, a suite of songs rather than a straightforward collection, something considerably more than its parts whose themes interpenetrate to plot the world of Ziggy Stardust, tragi-comic rock 'n' roll star, which is David Bowie's current identity. There is an inevitability about the appearance of Ziggy, especially within the corpus of Bowie's own work. A series of contemporary trends intersect to form an outrageously camped-up descendant of the mod: pretty, bitchy, vulnerable, excitable, shrewd, sometimes gentle, high adrenaline, freak in star-studded boots and dyed hair. Ziggy's combination of narcissism and defiance gives birth to the knave-queen, finding his kicks in a glossy urban landscape full of dramas."

"Bowie is no fool, he is not blind to the horrors of the

twilight zone, and its pain is an essential raw material for his songs. But he also knows that from this deadliness also derives the exhilaration. The scintillance and squalor of it provides the two poles between which, on this album, his music moves. It fuses the harshness of *The Man Who Sold The World* with the overt commercial panache of *Hunky Dory* to create an album which must do extremely well for Bowie. All the signs are that he is going to be very big indeed, and not before time. The schema of Ziggy Stardust is indefinite but not vague. The idea of a doomed beauty and hero-martyr predicates the album in the first cut, 'Five Years', a typical Bowie song with big romantic melody and chorus which at the outset admits the transience of the whole trip. Only five years. But of what? The world, the pop star, youth, fun? It doesn't matter. It would be all of these. The mood is right and sharpens the poignancy of what follows. This happens to be a beautiful teen pop song called 'Soul Love', all bittersweet, and high-pitched Bowie overdubs la-la-ing in the background."

"There is not much point in going through all the songs in sequence because they are moods, not items of narrative, and their arrangement is flexible. All have somewhere in them that elusive Bowie angst. None is underweight. Apart from large-scale production numbers like 'Lady Stardust', 'Starman', 'Ziggy Stardust', there is some truly frantic rock music on the album. 'Hang On To Yourself' has a fast riff swinging up and down, and manages to be both very original and terribly like the Velvet Underground at their best. Bowie intones the words in his exaggerated Lou Reed manner before breaking into a feline chorus which is all his own. Actually he intends to work with Reed soon which should produce some interesting permutations, even though Bowie has now overtaken Reed in almost every way."

"'Suffragette City' is faster still, a simple chromatic chord change providing the hook. Some of the songs incorporate

David Bowie - *The Rise And Fall Of Ziggy Stardust*

both aspects of Bowie, such as 'Moonage Daydream', which also has Mick Ronson stretching all his muscles on an aching aerial guitar solo. The end of the album, appropriately enough is 'Rock 'n' Roll Suicide', beginning in a subdued way and building to a shuddering climax which almost oversteps the mark. Only Bowie's aura of being larger than life, which I should call "theatrical realism" if I didn't feel that somewhere there must be a better way of describing it, can carry it off. The Spiders — Ronson (guitar and piano), Bolder (bass), Woodmansey (drums) — also help to keep the hard centre of the music from disintegrating under pressure from Bowie's imagination. Ronson's guitar is as dramatic and flashy as Bowie's metallic, twisting voice. He is also responsible for some of the arrangements, creating expansive effects without overloading the sound. The production too (Bowie and Ken Scott) generously takes advantage of the studio. There are a mass of tiny original details, little tit-bits for the ears, worked into the broad texture. This album celebrates a new social style as well — the volatile *Clockwork Orange* fag of inclusive tastes... We should soon see many sub-Bowies on the streets, his "Vaseline tigers". Curious that the album should come out at the same time as Burrough's novel, *The Wild Boys*. The general flavour of both is distinctly similar. A new cult is afoot."

From *Melody Maker*'s review in July 1972: "The cover of Bowie's new album has a picture of him in a telephone booth looking every inch the stylish poseur. Style and content have now become inextricably tangled in Bowie's case. Campness has become built-in to his public persona. I mean that, however, in a far from derogatory sense. The main preoccupation of David's work is not directly gay sexuality, though that element is there, as with a flourishing theatricality and dramatic sense. On *Ziggy Stardust* this is apparent even with a song like 'Five Years'. Ostensibly about the death of the world; Bowie turns it into a "performance" by virtue of his gift for artful mannerism and by creating a convincing mise-en-scène (a cop kneels at the feet of a priest and a soldier is run over by a car after it is announced on the news that the Earth has five years left). It would also go some way towards explaining why this album has such a conceptual sounding title. There is no well-defined story line, as there is in *Tommy* say, but there are odd songs and references to the business of being a pop star that overall add up to a strong sense of biographical drama."

"On one track 'Star' he sings about playing the wild mutation of a rock 'n' roll star. Then 'Ziggy Stardust', the title track, is about a guitar superhero who 'took it all too far'. The final track is simply called 'Rock 'n' Roll Suicide' — it speaks for itself. In the space of three songs he thus suggests the ascent and decline of a big rock figure, but leaves the listener to fill in his own details, and in the process he's also referring obliquely to his own role as a rock star and sending it up. There are many layers to Bowie the artist, but he has this uncanny knack of turning a whole album or stage performance into a torch song. *Ziggy Stardust* is a little less instantly appealing than *Hunky Dory*, basically because that album was written with the intention of being commercial. This one rocks more, though, and the paradox is that it will be much more commercially successful than the last, because Bowie's bid for stardom is accelerating at lightning speed."

From *Rolling Stone*: "Upon the release of David Bowie's most thematically ambitious, musically coherent album to date, the record in which he unites the major strengths of his previous work and comfortably reconciles himself to some apparently inevitable problems, we should all say a brief prayer that his fortunes are not made to rise and fall with the fate of the "drag-rock" syndrome — that thing that's manifesting itself in the self-conscious quest for decadence which is all the rage at the moment in trendy Hollywood, in the more contrived area of Alice Cooper's presentation, and, way down in the pits, in such grotesqueries as Queen, Nick St Nicholas' trio of feathered, sequined Barbie dolls. And which is bound to get worse."

"For although Lady Stardust himself has probably had more to do with androgyny's current fashionableness in rock than any other individual, he has never made his sexuality anything more than a completely natural and integral part of his public self, refusing to lower it to the level of gimmick but never excluding it from his image and craft. To do either would involve an artistically fatal degree of compromise. Which is not to say that he hasn't had a great time with it. Flamboyance and outrageousness are inseparable from that campy image of his, both in the Bacall and Garbo stages and in his new butch, street-crawler appearance that has him looking like something out of the darker pages of *City Of Night*. It's all tied up with the one aspect of David Bowie that sets him apart from both the exploiters of transvestitism and writers/performers of comparable talent — his theatricality."

"The news here is that he's managed to get that sensibility down on vinyl, not with an attempt at pseudo-visualism (which, as Mr Cooper has shown, just doesn't cut it), but through employment of broadly mannered styles and deliveries, a boggling variety of vocal nuances that provide the program with the necessary depth, a verbal acumen that is now more economic and no longer clouded by storms of psychotic, frenzied music, and, finally, a thorough command of the elements of rock and roll. It emerges as a series of concise vignettes designed strictly for the ear."

"Side two is the soul of the album, a kind of psychological equivalent of Lola vs. Powerman that delves deep into a matter close to David's heart: What's it all about to be a rock and roll star? It begins with a slow, fluid 'Lady Stardust', a song in which currents of frustration and triumph merge in an overriding desolation. For though 'He was alright…', still 'People stared at the makeup on his face'. The pervading bittersweet melancholy that wells out of the contradictions and that Bowie beautifully captures with one of the album's more direct vocals conjures the picture of a painted harlequin under the spotlight of a deserted theatre in the darkest hour of the night. 'Star' springs along handsomely as he confidently tells us that 'I could make it all worthwhile as a rock and roll star'. Here Bowie outlines the dazzling side of the coin: 'So inviting — so enticing to play the part.' His singing is a delight, full of mocking intonations and backed way down in the mix with excessive, marvellously designed 'Ooooohh la la la's and such that are both a joy to listen to and part of the parodic undercurrent that runs through the entire album."

"'Hang On To Yourself' is both a kind of warning and an irresistible erotic rocker (especially the hand-clapping chorus), and apparently Bowie has decided that since he just can't avoid cramming too many syllables into his lines, he'll simply master the rapid-fire, tongue-twisting phrasing that his failing requires. 'Ziggy Stardust' has a faint ring of *The Man Who Sold The World* to it — stately, measured, fuzzily electric. A tale of intra-group jealousies, it features some of Bowie's more adventuresome imagery, some of which is really the nazz: 'So we bitched about his fans and should we crush his sweet hands?'"

"David Bowie's supreme moment as a rock and roller is 'Suffragette City', a relentless, spirited Velvet Underground — styled rushing of chomping guitars. When that second layer of guitar roars in on the second verse you're bound to be a goner, and that priceless little break at the end — a sudden cut to silence from a mighty crescendo, Bowie's voice oozing out as a brittle, charged 'Oooohh Wham Bam Thank You Ma'am!' followed hard by two raspy guitar bursts that suck you back in to the surging meat of the chorus — will surely make your tum do somersaults. And as for our Star, well, now 'There's only room for one and here she comes, here she comes.' But the price of playing the part must be paid, and we're precipitously tumbled into the quietly terrifying despair of 'Rock 'n' Roll Suicide'. The broken singer drones: 'Time takes a cigarette...' But there is a way out of the bleakness, and it's realised with Bowie's Lennon-like scream: 'You're not alone...'. It rolls on to a tumultuous, impassioned climax, and though the mood isn't exactly sunny, a desperate, possessed optimism asserts itself as genuine, and a new point from which to climb is firmly established."

"Side one is certainly less challenging, but no less enjoyable from a musical standpoint. Bowie's favourite themes — Mortality ('Five Years', 'Soul Love'), the necessity of reconciling oneself to Pain (those two and 'It Ain't Easy'), the New Order vs. the Old in sci-fi garments ('Starman') are presented with a consistency, a confidence, and a strength in both style and technique that were never fully realised in the lashing *The Man Who Sold The World* or the uneven and too often stringy *Hunky Dory*. Bowie imitates 'Moonage Daydream' on side one with a riveting bellow of 'I'm an alligator' that's delightful in itself but which also has a lot to do with what *Rise And Fall...* is all about. Because in it there's the perfect touch of self-mockery, a lusty but forlorn bravado that is the first hint of the central duality and of the rather spine-tingling questions that rise from it: Just how big and tough is your rock and roll star? How much of him is bluff and how much inside is very frightened and helpless? And is this what comes of our happily dubbing someone as "bigger than life"?"

"David Bowie has pulled off his complex task with consummate style, with some great rock and roll (The Spiders are Mick Ronson on guitar and piano, Mick Woodmansey on drums and Trevor Bolder on bass; they're good), with all the wit and passion required to give it sufficient dimension and with a deep sense of humanity that regularly emerges from behind the star facade. The important thing is that despite the formidable nature of the undertaking, he hasn't sacrificed a bit of entertainment value for the sake of message. I'd give it at least a ninety-nine."

Terry Atkinson reviewed the album for *Phonograph Record Magazine* in July 1972; "Turn and face the strange changes. Like — ho, ho, look out you rock 'n' rollers. Apocalypse. Is rock and roll the baby of the current apocalyptic concept, with its supermarket variety of possible manifestations? How's it gonna come? When's it gonna come? Marc Bolan says he's got less than ten years to live. David Bowie gives everyone five, tops. In the meantime: The Last Mad Dash... the hanged man's hard-on. Boys, toys, electric irons and TVs, a girl my age went off her head, cops, Cadillac's, news guys, violence, sex, dope and rock 'n' roll! Which just gets zippier and zippier, especially when the blokes doing it think they're gonna die soon — this is the end — so that you get just-in-case-this-is-the-last-one ultimate works of art and craziness like David Bowie's *The Rise And Fall Of Ziggy Stardust And The Spiders From Mars*. Uh huh."

"Bowie's rampant schizoid brilliance is along the same zig-zag lines as that of the artists he admires: Lou Reed, Marc Bolan, Iggy Stooge, Syd Barrett. And like that of some others he may or may not admire: Vincent Van Gogh, R. Meltzer, William Burroughs, Don Rickles, Ken Russell, Wild Man Fisher, Kim Fowley, Jackson Pollock, Ludwig Van Beethoven. Men whose conscious states hover around the line between genius and madness, between creativity and a wild, scattered sort of super-perception, some slightly on one side of the lines, others just across it on the opposite side, many flying back and forth. Bowie, with his last three albums, and especially with *Ziggy*, has implanted himself quite solidly on the genius-creative side. And yet he has not strayed too far from the line: the wildness is still there. Unlike Van Gogh and Barrett, he has not let his ardour burn without control and self-care; and unlike Bolan, he has not allowed a system of order to cramp his powers. And David Bowie's just as smashing on his album. Why not? After all he is Ziggy Stardust, the rock 'n' roll Starman."

"Actually to be Ziggy, who "really sang" and played that guitar that way, sort of your total fave-rave, Bowie — being in some respects mortal — called on the help of his own Spiders From Mars, and boy can they play. In the Drone-Chord-Riff Olympics of '72 Mick Ronson, the man behind the man on Bowie's last three albums, might have to give up the gold and silver medals to Townshend and Page, but I think he'd be a good bet for third place over the other competitors who come to mind (even Beck, Iommi and Blackmore). Bowie and then-producer (and bass player) Tony Visconti gave Ronson practically free rein on *The Man Who Sold The World*, and Mick (not unlike Bowie at the time) came off erratic — mostly brilliant but sometimes sounding completely lost. So on *Hunky Dory* he got a muzzle put on him and he plunked away most humbly except on 'Queen Bitch'. *Ziggy* is for him, as well as Bowie, a peak of effectivity. Mick Woodmansey has also been along for the ride and is too better than ever sounding much like the clean ratatat of T. Rex's drummer which is just fine. When Bowie and Visconti severed ties after *Man*, Trevor Bolder was added on bass, and he's up to it. *The Man Who Sold The World*, *Hunky Dory*, and *Ziggy Stardust* have proven David Bowie to be the Master of the Nice Touch. The albums are jam packed with Nice Touches, and you put enough of those together, and you've got immortal music (Bowie's first two albums, *Love You Till Tuesday* — also issued as *The World Of David Bowie* — and *David Bowie*, are merely good). For example, the crowning Nice Touch used to be the superbly haunting repetitive code: the 'zane, zane, zane — ouvre le chien' of 'All The Madmen' on *Man* and the 'please come away' of the 'Bewlay Brothers' (on *Hunky*), sung by a multi-multi-voiced Bowie (he always does all the voices, which represent varying characters in imitation or spirit evocation) in what must be the most purely mystical and brain-melting fade-outs in all of rockdom. The best batch of many types of Nice Touches on *Ziggy* is the Perfect Rock Exclamation. David always knows just at what time, and with what volume, and with what tone to deliver an 'oh yeah' or 'oh' or 'ooh' or whelp or sigh. He makes his own alterations and amendments to traditional interjections too, as with the substitute for 'one more time' in 'Suffragette City': 'Wham Bam Thank You Ma'am'. Note also the magnetised swishy-brat two-syllable repetitions that serve as the matrix of 'Suffragette City' ('hey man') and 'Hang On To Yourself' ('come on'). Neo classic. Which shows in the structure, too. Some of the songs, as in the past, are homages, semi-imitations, employments of admitted styles: The Who in 'Star' (hear the 'Pinball Wizard' opening?), Jan and Dean and the Beach Boys in 'Suffragette City', T. Rex and Ray Davies and Velvet Underground and who else in 'Hang On To Yourself' among others."

"And, it's a concept album! The story of how into a despairing, dying world, a star from the stars and his band come and thrill all and then Ziggy gets bumped off — rock 'n' roll assassination — by envious/adoring fans. Actually, only the second side is story proper. Though the songs on the first side relate, they are mainly separate entities. Side one is made up of five excellent if somewhat subdued songs which serve as a tasty prelude to the almost continually zapping second side and even go beyond the role of appetiser in two cases: 'Soul Love', which is a description of how love is all important, multiform, and too often degenerate ('idiot love') yet not without worth even in that form, set in a lovely and haunting melody and featuring a Bowie plastic-sax solo; and 'Starman', a blissfully hopeful ballad-boogie about a very modern mystical revelation (via radio!), with a scrumptiously Ronson guitar tune following the vocals twice, lastly to so gorgeously fade. The other three songs on side one are the album opener, 'Five Years' stating

David Bowie - *The Rise And Fall Of Ziggy Stardust*

the despair that gives excuse for ecstatic creation as well as tears, thereby setting the scene: 'Moonage Daydream', a sci-fi sex three-quarter-speed rocker — very spacey electronic echoes and squeaks; and the only non-Bowie-penned song Ron Davies' 'It Ain't Easy' well done indeed but a slight mistake as an end to side one, seemingly a filler after 'Starman's right finish fadeout."

"Then side two: on one level, Ziggy's story; on another, hopeful/fearful autobiography. 'Lady Stardust' is the wondrous image of the rock star, the composer-singer-player, as animus (his animal grace) and anima ('Lady Stardust' sang his songs of darkness and disgrace) and animus (he sang all night long) all mixed up with beauty and without care. The song is a ballad-tempo prelude to four straight super-rockers: 'Star'. THIS IS IT. The first three seconds tell you this is the kind of song that rock's all about. Absolute energy and happiness. A nonchalantly ambitious song about how nice it might be to be a rock 'n' roll star. Well it would be a change... Knock-you-off-your-seat stops and starts, tap-dancing-up-and-down-the-stairs drums punctuated by the fluffiest rolls, and finally: 'I could fall asleep at night...'. Watch him now?! What's he been doing for the last three minutes?! Anyway, it's on to 'Hang On To Yourself' a taste of what Ziggy and The Spiders From Mars could lay down before Zig got bumped off. Zowie. Tigers on Vaseline. 'Ziggy Stardust', the song slows things down only slightly to summarise the story of Ziggy's talents and assassination, told from at least two view points — one of The Spiders' and one of the assassin's. Still rockin'. And even after Zig's demise we get another example of his hits; or you can fit in that way anyhow, if you're concerned with structure. This is 'Suffragette City', a dizzying classic. 'Rock 'n' Roll Suicide' is the Tony Newley/'Bewlay Brothers' wind-up to the whole thing, with an uplifting ending ('You're not alone, gimme your hands!') that's a little too strident to be taken completely seriously and little too truthful to have its conviction totally dismissed. *Ziggy* is the perfection in popular recorded sound."

Also in July 1972, John Tiven wrote of the album for the same publication; "David Bowie, England's Answer-To-Alice-Cooper-But-He's-For-Real, has finally made an album with positive commercial potential and consistent strength. *Ziggy Stardust* is the aftermath of the seventies, where every track is a hit and no fillers; what's more Bowie is with his band and rocking at the seams of his kelly-green jumpsuit all the way down to his screwed down hairdo. Bowie's tale is of a rock star from start to finito, and is pretty all-inclusive: screaming teenies, frantic groupies, envious band members, et cetera. There are no bad songs on this album, just great songs and good ones."

"There has been a single released, 'Starman' and it's the fusion of all mod British pop and 'Somewhere Over the Rainbow'. Bowie has a way with words, uses keen phrases like 'leper messiah', 'hazy cosmic jive' and 'tongue twisting storm.' 'Starman's chorus features the absolute most exquisite pronunciation of 'boogie' ever, rhymes it with 'loose it'. The band is marvellous, from the tone of Mick Ronson's electric guitar to the bass lines of Trevor Bolder. The production is outstanding, even for Bowie (whose previous albums haven't been bad either, mind you). Strings are used sparingly, arrangements are complex but come across as simple pop rock. This album is obviously one of the finest records released this year, but even more importantly, this is the most universally enjoyable disc in a long time. Play *Ziggy* for hippies, mods, AM'ers, they'll all like it. Hell, my mother asked me to play it again when I gave it a spin in the downstairs living room, and I wouldn't be surprised if she bought herself a copy. Anyway, my high school graduation is this year and what a perfect record to remember as being from my seventeenth and a half year on this planet!"

David Bowie - *The Rise And Fall Of Ziggy Stardust*

In the same feature, Jim Bickhart advocated; "Since jumping from Mercury to RCA, David Bowie has added the decipherable touch to his recordings which they needed to reach more than the esoteric crew of rock critics that his two Mercury albums were embraced by. Consequently the newer records *Hunky Dory* and now *Ziggy Stardust* are selling and Bowie is ripping up English audiences with a stage show designed to embarrass everyone from T. Rex to The Cockettes. Five years ago, Bowie was making typically English rock and roll story records, his image late-sixties flash mod flower phase child. He then moved on to poetry and art rock, going through a semi-acoustic and an odd hit record called 'Space Oddity', which reflected both his interests in rebelliousness and intergalactic matters. Next came some very electric, at times almost heavy-metal psychotic commentary by way of a powerful album called *The Man Who Sold The World*."

"*Ziggy Stardust*, the outgrowth of Bowie's new openness is a self-contained rock and roll album about rock and roll. Bowie's band, guitarist Mick Ronson, bassist Trevor Bolder and drummer Mick Woodmansey, team with the singer-guitarist to both perform and play the roles depicted in the album's songs: to a limited extent, they are Ziggy Stardust and The Spiders From Mars. And most certainly they are an excellent rock band. The songs, beginning with the doom-portending 'Five Years', creates a tale in which a number of Bowie's beliefs and fantasies are placed in full view. The thread of the plot goes from the announcement of impending doom through the uncontrollability of love ('Soul Love') to a major turning point, 'Moonage Daydream', where Ziggy, whoever he is before he actually becomes Ziggy, is zapped by a combination of religion (first invoked at the end of 'Soul Love'), romance, rock and roll and bisexuality. Symbolically it is probably the album's most important number."

"From this point, the new rock and roll idol, ostensibly

an invader from space (though it is really space in someone's imagination), begins making himself public. 'Starman' presents his arrival on Earth both as a physical phenomenon and as a religious occurrence. A stylised rendition of Ron Davies' funky 'It Ain't Easy' takes Ziggy on a sexual tangent to finish side one. Side two is more directly devoted to the rise and fall of Ziggy and The Spiders. 'Lady Stardust' says, in no uncertain terms, that this rock star appeals sexually to everyone in the audience, just as it is actually the case with most superstars (Bowie, though, has a way of not mincing his words). 'Star' offers the singer's motivation for seeking fame, and 'Hang On To Yourself' describes the position of the band as they begin to discover the nature of their appeal and precisely what they must do to make it big. 'Ziggy Stardust' compresses, in rock ballad form, the basic story of the band's fling with stardom."

"The final pair of numbers, the ballsy 'Suffragette City' and 'Rock 'n' Roll Suicide' are a bit anti-climatic in content. 'Suffragette City' is pure lust and out of sequence (it would seem more comfortable if heard before the idea of Ziggy's downfall is introduced), though it is the album's classic rocker in the Rolling Stones sense. 'Suicide' is a symbolic reference for the idea of what the forgotten idol does after the fall. David Bowie, on the strength of his five albums, is certainly one of the more distinctive personalities in rock, and that alone is enough to make his very listenable records a bit extra-ordinary. Even if some of his ideas don't quite work out, his talent for strong conception and sound execution is undeniable. Should he become a star of Ziggy Stardust magnitude, he will deserve it, and hopefully his daydreams won't be forced to turn to suicide when it's all over."

Beat Instrumental wrote in September 1972; "Bowie's albums seem to possess that strange quality which allow them to 'grow' on the listener over a period of time. Coupled with a visit to a live concert of his, the effect can be devastating!

David Bowie - *The Rise And Fall Of Ziggy Stardust*

Now that Bowie has settled in with his band, the albums are becoming less studio-oriented and establish him as a rock 'n' roll singer pure and straight. Side two is a chronicle of his life as a 'star' ending with contemplation on 'Rock 'n' Roll Suicide'. The strongest numbers on the album are 'Starman', 'Hang On To Yourself' and his favourite encore raver 'Suffragette City'. Definitely an album for every serious rock fan. A taste of things to come."

UK

UK

The photo of Bowie was taken – just off Regent Street – on Heddon Street, London, W1. It has gone on to become one of the most iconic covers of all time.

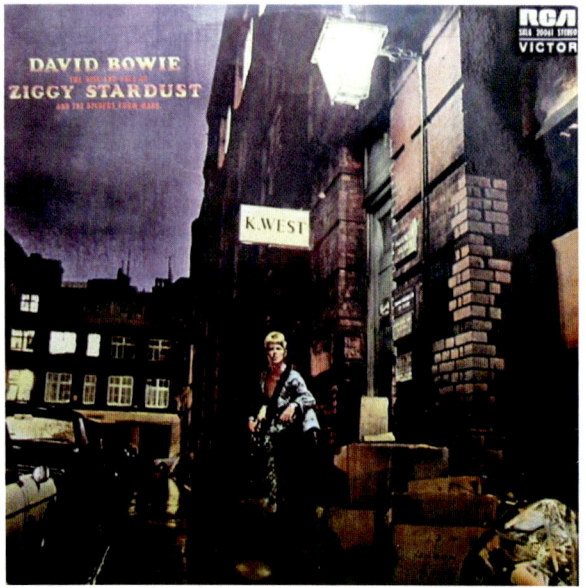

Greece

Greece

The cover photo was actually shot in monochrome and then colourised. This might explain why there were sleeve variants such as this version from Greece. RCA Greece also decided to have a different back cover design though.

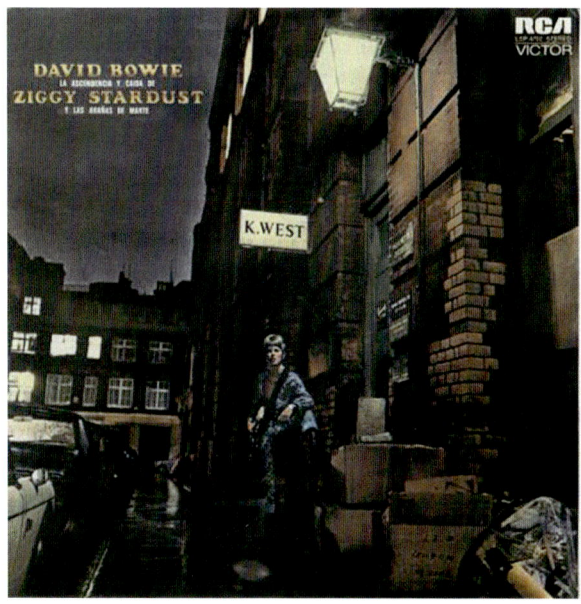

Spain

Spain

Another variant, this one from Spain, where the title is in Spanish, while the standard back cover has a blue tint.

Venezuela

Venezuela

In Venezuela the cover declared that the album was presented by journalist, entertainer and radio host Napoleon Bravo. It was quite common for Venezuela to promote albums alongside well-known nationals. The back cover was simply reproduced in monochrome.

UK

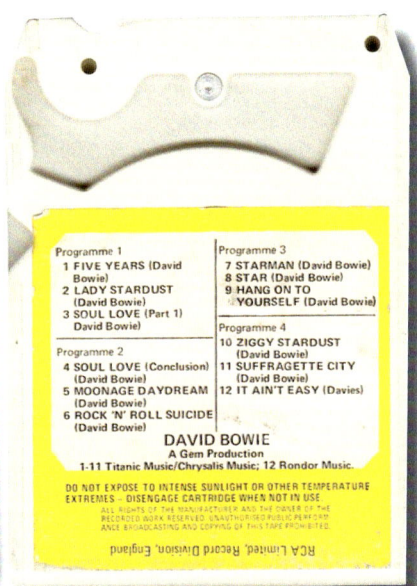

UK

USA

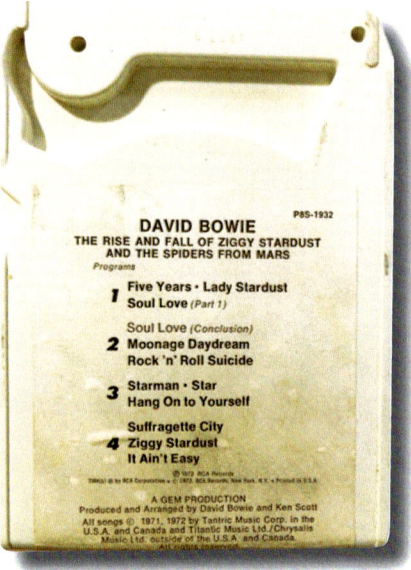

USA

The 8-track cartridge format was popular at the time, particularly in the States, despite the fact that the format resulted in changes to how the tracks were presented.

The rectangular design of cassettes always had a habit of offering up lots of variants around the world.

France

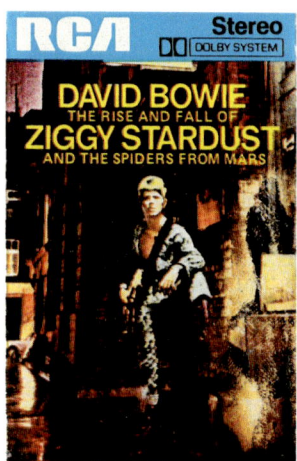
Italy

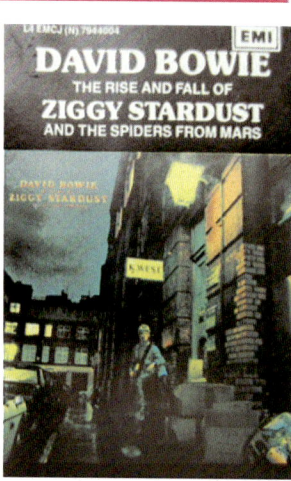
Greece

Spain

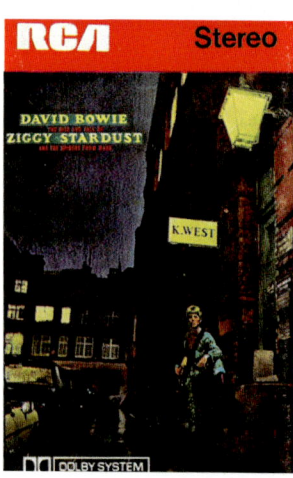
South Africa

UK

'Starman' was selected as the single. In Portugal it was released as a four-track EP. In Italy and Spain it was coupled with the non-album track 'John, I'm Only Dancing'.

Elsewhere 'Suffragette City' was the B-side. Picture sleeve singles were still not the norm in the UK and the USA at the time but were commonplace elsewhere. Most countries settled for a monochrome photo of David, but Japan had its own unique design.

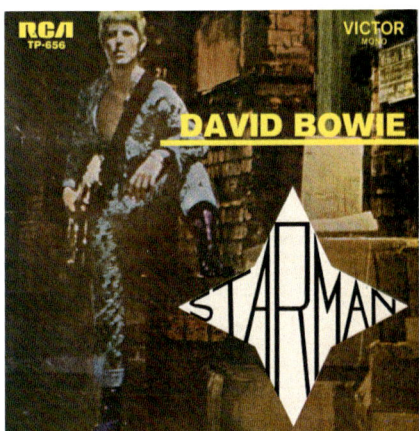

Portugal

Italy

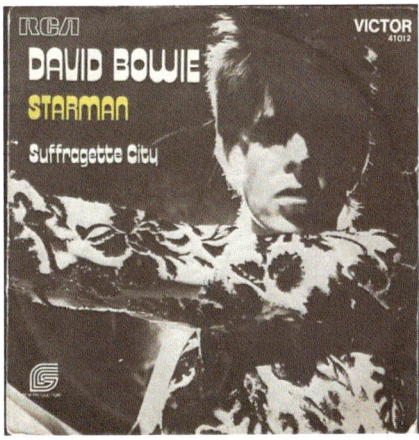

France

Japan

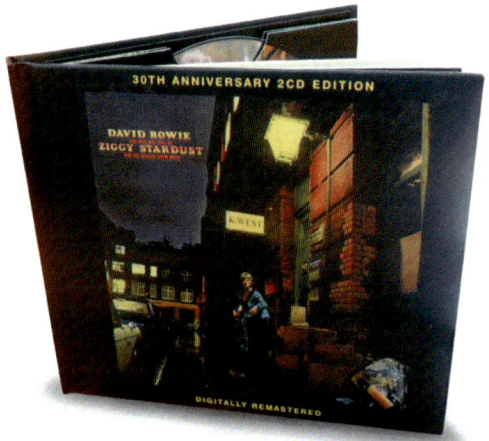

The advent of CD in the eighties ensured the album's longevity and in 2002 it was given the deluxe, expanded treatment.

The iconic status of the Ziggy Stardust album is illustrated in the use of the cover on this rare, extremely limited-edition, 2007 Japanese CD box set release that features the six albums from David Bowie (aka Space Oddity) to Pinups in mini LP-replica sleeves with lyrics & obi-strips.

Chapter Three

Live Performances

Prior to their January 1972 debut at Friars Aylesbury, Bowie had taken The Spiders to see *A Clockwork Orange*. He explained to them that the film's costumes (designed by Milena Canonero) were not something to feel uncomfortable wearing, but futuristic. Upon being presented with the costumes that they were to wear on stage (designed by Freddie Burretti who had previously been part of the Arnold Corns project), The Spiders were not happy about it. Persuasive and determined though, Bowie managed to convince them all to play along.

A favourite venue, it was back to Friars Aylesbury on 15th July 1972. *Cash Box* reported of the performance that month; "Contrary to what you might read in some of the papers, David Bowie is not Cleopatra, a powdered chameleon, a dewy-eyed Space Waif or a child from the Village of the Damned. He is not even a personification of Ziggy Stardust. Last weekend when his concert act was on display for representatives of the American music press at this club near London, it was apparent, though, almost from the start, that what Bowie is, is a damned good rock and roller. That is not to say that Bowie isn't daring. But his audacity is less in his appearance or even in his stage behaviour than in the contents and the thrust of his songs. Always a skilful ('Love You Till Tuesday') and imaginative ('Space Oddity') composer, Bowie, in the past year or so, has become an important chronicler of twentieth century madness and an energetic prophesier of events still to come. And he has

David Bowie - *The Rise And Fall Of Ziggy Stardust*

encased all of the brilliance of his lyrics and inventiveness of his melodies in the basic jacket of rock and roll. Accompanied by his group, The Spiders From Mars, Bowie offered a liberal sampling of tunes from his two RCA albums, interspersing them with a few of his vintage pieces and beautiful interpretations of two such diverse songs as Brel's 'Port Of Amsterdam' and the old Cream goodie, 'I Feel Free'. For now I'll just say that it was a vivid glittering set."

The same Aylesbury performance was reviewed by *Record World* in August; "Before a hand-picked panel of American press in various stages of readiness for his glittering lubricity, and more importantly, before an enthusiastic throng of rock-mad teens, David Bowie made that most essential transition from "recording artist" to "Stardom Incarnate" at the Aylesbury Friars, a small club outside of London where Bowie chose to finish up his most successful tour of England yet. That David's words have become most appealing flesh cannot be denied, his bedazzling chameleon jumpsuit allowing for no busted buttons, though the merest hint of a codpiece implied that nature does indeed follow art. Bowie's act, despite its flash and finesse, cleaves close to the material itself, rearranging the Bowie repertoire to highlight the special talents of The Spiders — the platinum blond and electrifying Mick Ronson on guitar and the tightly knit, bottomly round rhythm section of Mick Woodmansey and Trevor Bolder. Using the epic *Ziggy Stardust* LP as a framework, Bowie's performances as a vocalist and acoustic guitarist are stylish rather than arbitrarily "spontaneous". Pantomimic gestures and changes of facial expression add running comments to such recent favourites as 'Lady Stardust' and 'Life On Mars' whilst on acoustic numbers like 'Space Oddity' and 'Port Of Amsterdam', Bowie's excellence as a rock actor made for hushed attention. If the success of *Ziggy* as a top twenty chart item has created new audiences for Bowie, his show itself is nothing less than a

Live Performances

varied and flexible picture of the man as a complete and durable artist. Bowie makes the transitions between numbers like his own 'Queen Bitch' and Cream's 'I Feel Free' seem as natural as changing his outfit, which he manages at least once during the act with little ostentation and great effect. Aylesbury Friars is a small venue long accustomed to welcoming up and coming British bands but it seems likely that America, with its larger halls and perhaps more sceptical audiences, will bring David Bowie and The Spiders to such a high degree of finish that live performance may yet again come into its own as a medium designed to provide experience itself rather than a mere visual souvenir of an audio track memorised by every ticket holder. If Bowie's act is stylised it is nevertheless too scintillating and physically powerful to permit a programmed response from the listener. I guess it's true what they say about red-haired, crew-cut pop stars. Wait and see for yourself."

One of the most famous of Bowie's appearances on the Ziggy Stardust tour was at London's Rainbow Theatre on 19th August 1972. In his use of theatrics and multi-media, Bowie's live performances were considered to be ahead of their time. The gig at the Rainbow was certainly demonstrative of that.

By August 1972, the *Ziggy Stardust* album had only been released just two months earlier. Bowie's 7:30pm performance at the Rainbow was his first performance after a month's break following the earlier shows on the Ziggy Stardust tour. With the Rainbow being able to seat 3,000, it signified the point at which the tour's gigs were no longer confined to just smaller venues. Amazingly, the date at the Rainbow was initially going to be the final date of Bowie's UK tour. Once the tickets for the date had sold out within two hours though, another date was booked at the Rainbow for the following night. It too sold out quickly. Following this success, Bowie would go on to play a further ten dates on his UK tour. With the last of the ten being in Bristol on 27th August, Bowie maintained that the extra shows were

simply "warm ups" in preparation for the US leg of the tour.
The Rainbow performance was promoted in the *New Musical Express* gig guide as follows: "Hello handsome, my name's David and I'm going to be at the Rainbow in lovely North London with The Spiders From Mars, some very pretty people called Roxy Music and a gorgeous butch blues singer called Lloyd Watson this Saturday and Sunday. It would be just too, too divine if you could make it there — and if you can't make it there just be there hmmm? It's going to be the most exquisite concert of the year."

Prior to their performance at the Rainbow, Bowie and The Spiders rehearsed for a fortnight at the Theatre Royal in East Stafford. Bowie's former mime teacher Lindsay Kemp was there to help with the choreography. Kemp had been invited by Bowie's wife Angie as a matter of last-minute urgency. Kemp brought four other dancers with him to work on the show. They performed under the name of The Astronettes. Kemp himself appeared as the character of Starman on stage. In later years, Kemp claimed that his twelve-person mime act was also invited to tour the US with Bowie as a continuation of the Rainbow stage show. It was apparently due to financial limitations that this never happened.

Dress-designer Natasha Korniloff was called in to make ten white elastic bodysuits. Angie Bowie arranged the light show. The day before the performance at the Rainbow, Bowie told a journalist; "I think what I do and the way I dress is me pandering to my own eccentricities and imagination. It's a continual fantasy. Nowadays there is really no difference between my personal life and anything I do on stage. I'm very rarely David Jones anymore. I think I've forgotten who David Jones is."

Apparently, a Japanese film crew was invited to film the concert. With no footage ever having been released though, this is uncertain. Additionally, security at the Rainbow was so

Live Performances

strict that night that only one photographer from *Melody Maker* was allowed to take photographs. Although some parts of the show were documented — both on audio tape and video — by concert goers, the quality of such footage is of a disappointingly low quality.

On the day of the first performance at the Rainbow, Bowie and The Spiders rehearsed all afternoon. Some of this was filmed and used as part of the video for the song, 'John, I'm Only Dancing' (which was released as a single in September 1972). Wearing fishnet string costumes designed by Lindsay Kemp, The Astronettes also appear in this video.

A fold-out promotional flyer was given out to members of the audience. It featured a miniature of the *Ziggy Stardust* album's front and back cover.

Blues guitarist Lloyd Watson and the yet-to-be-well-known Roxy Music were the opening acts for the two Rainbow dates. In the audience and excited to support Bowie on the first night was Elton John, Alice Cooper, Mick Jagger and Rod Stewart.

Although the details of the second Rainbow date were not as liberally documented at the time, it is a likelihood that the set list was similar on both nights:

A Clockwork Orange Theme
Lady Stardust
Hang On To Yourself
Ziggy Stardust
Life On Mars?
The Supermen
Changes
Five Years
Space Oddity
Andy Warhol
My Death
The Width Of A Circle

David Bowie - *The Rise And Fall Of Ziggy Stardust*

The Wild Eyed Boy From Freecloud
Starman
Queen Bitch
Suffragette City
White Light/White Heat
Waiting For The Man
Concluding Speech
Encore — Moonage Daydream

When asked about how, when playing live, he didn't do the songs from side two in the same order that they appear on the *Ziggy Stardust* record, Bowie told *New Musical Express* in July 1972; "I must admit I speculate on the prospect of a show which would be *Ziggy Stardust*, but the way I want to do it requires a lot of planning and we haven't had time for that. I'd rather leave it alone until it's gonna be done properly. I don't want to do anything unless it's gonna be done well."

As the Walter (later Wendy) Carlos *Clockwork Orange* theme played, Bowie walked enigmatically out of the darkness, surrounded by an abundance of dry ice, and with a twelve-string guitar ready to perform 'Lady Stardust' as the opening number.

As one journalist described it, "When the spotlights come on, the audience gives up a single gasp of utter disbelief. Ziggy's hair is a solid bob of flaming apricot gold, made even brighter by a deathly white made-up face. He is wearing a blue Lurex jacket open to the navel and a pair of blue denims tucked into what appears to be boxing boots. The Spiders... seem ill at ease in their silver jumpsuits. The exhibition that follows is of secondary importance. David Bowie made his impact the second he stood there under the lamp, legs apart, hips gently swaying, guitar slung over his back and a limp smile playing on his mouth. There's no getting away from it, the boy is beautiful."

As Bowie sang 'Lady Stardust', amongst others, an image

of Marc Bolan was projected onto the left of the stage. Also during this number, The Astronettes wore David Bowie masks.

Bowie's use of the stage at the Rainbow was extensive. He took advantage of the many levels of scaffolding following a costume change. He was able to do this with the connecting ladders available. It allowed him the scope to appear either above or below the dancers.

Bowie first changed costume after performing 'Changes'. Mick Woodmansey played a drum solo as part of the beginning of 'Five Years' in order to buy Bowie some time in which to do this.

It was after performing 'Andy Warhol' that Bowie addressed the audience directly: "This is a Jacques Brel number, but it's not 'Port Of Amsterdam'. It's equally as cheerful and it's called 'My Death'."

During his performance of 'Starman', Bowie changed the lyrics to acknowledge the Rainbow: "There's a Starman... over the rainbow."

After his performance of two Lou Reed songs — 'White Light/White Heat' and 'Waiting For The Man' — Bowie addressed the audience: "I'd like to thank you for coming to our little show tonight. I'd like to thank The Astronettes for dancing it, I'd like to thank Trevor Bolder, Woody Woodmansey and Mick Ronson — The Spiders, for playing it. Thanks to my guest artist Mr Lindsay Kemp and lastly, I'd like to thank you. Thank you and good night."

Used as the encore song, Bowie introduced 'Moonage Daydream': "This is one of Ziggy's numbers."

The success of the gigs at the Rainbow, along with the positive critical acclaim, resulted in a sharp increase in sales of the *Ziggy Stardust* album.

A witness told *Melody Maker* in August 1972; "On that evening, I arrived during the closing minutes of Roxy Music's support act. I had no idea what to expect (it was a work colleague's idea to attend the concert) but I was quite excited as there was an unusually expectant atmosphere building up in the auditorium. A short while later this was cut by taped music from *Clockwork Orange* followed by an extract of the fourth movement of Beethoven's Ninth Symphony played by Matthew Fisher (formerly of Procol Harum) on an off-stage organ. During this, the orange-haired Bowie, in green patterned jumpsuit and long, silver boots walked slowly forward from the gloomy rear of the stage, strumming his twelve-string guitar. The Spiders had already assumed their positions, and as the organ stopped Bowie's now audible strumming led the band into the opening number. The stage set was fairly simple, yet innovative of the time, being constructed of scaffolding, framed by ladders at either side of the stage, and containing a screen off-centre to the left on which obscure clips of black and white film were shown from time to time to complete various songs. The whole stage was covered in sawdust (stardust?) and had a group of three dancers (The Astronettes) dressed in fishnet body stockings in the background. What was used was used with the utmost effectiveness, but the production was actually put together on a shoe-string budget, an example of which was Bowie's hand movements to replace the as-yet unaffordable synthesiser in the lift-off sequence of 'Space Oddity'."

"Halfway through the show, Bowie left the stage while The Spiders played an instrumental number. A few moments later he re-appeared in a scant, red and yellow tunic, high up on a catwalk atop the scaffolding. When he climbed back down to the stage his study of mime became apparent during the sequence where he seemed to be feeling his way, with the palms of his hands, along an invisible wall. Appearing to find a narrow gap, he pushed his fingers through and gave the impression of terrific strain as he tried to push the two sections of the wall apart. Just when he seemed about to escape, the invisible wall snapped shut again with Ziggy still on the other

Live Performances

side of it. At this point I left my seat in the circle and went downstairs. I walked down the central aisle of the stalls until I was level with the front row, then couched to the right of another person taking photos. After taking nearly a dozen pictures, suddenly a burly coloured man ran towards me. Wildly gesturing with his arm that I should stop what I was doing and get back. Clutching my Pentax, I ran back to my seat. Only later did I find out that for reasons of managerial strategy only one photographer (from *Melody Maker*) had been given permission to take photographs. Throughout the performance, Bowie held the audience spellbound with every enunciated word and choreographed movement. He allowed himself no unstaged actions (e.g. scratch an itch or take liquid refreshments); he didn't even announce the songs. And for those he hadn't already won over, the twenty-five-year-old who had walked on as a singer, walked off as a star."

Chris Welch's review was printed in *Melody Maker* the following week; "Music from *A Clockwork Orange* heralded the spectacular performance staged by David Bowie at London's Rainbow Theatre on Sunday night. 'At least it makes a change from *2001*' was one ruffianly comment noted as the stardust began to fall. There was an intensity and well-rehearsed devotion to detail evident in the theatrics to come that reminded one of *The Talk Of The Town*. In truth it was often tremendously effective. Mr Bowie's grand entrance, clad in a suit of silver with matching boots, he strode out with perfect timing to ankle-deep jets of smoke. A yelp and a scream came from the expectant audience. Great cheers greeted the familiar opening chords to songs, and of course the whole evening could be judged a wondrous success."

"But eventually the faint suspicion grew that certain sections of the audience were slightly stunned and bemused by the jive David was laying on us. After the final moments of wild balletic freak-out with the star arching his limbs in best

David Bowie - *The Rise And Fall Of Ziggy Stardust*

Nureyev fashion, there was a stunned silence. Then one lone voice bawled out 'more!' and taking their cue the audience gave the required ovation. It seemed like an extravagantly long show, and David and his management took a lot of risks in unleashing such a novel mixing of medias. In the old days they would have called it: Professional suicide. But these days chaps — well anything goes. In his rock-theatre venture the Big D was joined by a team of inventive dancers whose doll-like movements recalled some of the Arthur Brown's early experiments with neck bending... The Spiders From Mars played a brilliant backing role... there was created a dramatic, absorbing play upon the emotions."

"One of the most memorable moments, one that shall ever live on in my consciousness, came when David appeared in natty red underwear on the highest platform, there to strike unnatural poses, while bathed in soft lighting. The silver suit discarded, there were some moments of uncertainty. Was it he? But yes of course, as the microphone was raised, so that familiar voice boomed overhead, and a cold tingle of recognition tingled the kneecaps. As 'Starman' rocked on, a glittering mirrored globe began to revolve in the best patois fashion and the Star Man represented by a geezer in wings, lit up a fag and joined some brisk mixed dancing. David joined them on the ground floor, his legs freed from the encumbrance of trousers in order that he might participate in the final, exultant dance of lunacy. It would be hard to imagine audiences as long as three weeks ago, accepting such a spectacle without recourse to raspberries and maybe even yells of 'get on with it'. But times change rapidly in the rock business, God knows what will be happening next week. The triumph was David Bowie's and he has obviously come a long way since whatever he was doing last year. Whether all this folderol can survive the summer remains to be seen, but by God it has brought a little glamour into all our lives and Amen to that."

Live Performances

It was in the same month that *New Musical Express* reviewed the performance; "David Bowie's show is definitely a spectacular in the grand tradition. A Bowie concert is your real old Busby Berkeley production. Bring on the dancing girls — or rather The Astronettes with Lindsay Kemp, wheel on the dry ice machine and put some mystique back into the whole deal... Lou Reed later described Bowie's set as 'amazing, incredible, stupendous — the greatest thing I've ever seen'. While Lou is not exactly the most impartial of observers on things Bowie, he knows a good show when he sees one, and this was perhaps the most consciously theatrical rock show ever staged — and, by and by, it made Alice (Cooper) look like a third form dramatic society."

"With a multi-level stage, a light show, sawdust on the floor, The Spiders in all their glory and backstage Matthew Fisher playing piano, it could hardly fail and it didn't. Right from his entrance walking through a cloud of dry ice up to the microphone to sing 'Lady Stardust' (while the face of Marc Bolan was projected onto a screen by his side) Bowie provided a thoroughly convincing demonstration of his ascendancy over any other soloist in rock today. With perhaps the finest body of work of any contemporary songwriter, and the resources to perform this work to its utmost advantage, there really isn't anything going that tops the current Ziggy show. Other more basic performances have got me off more and higher — Hendrix, The Dead, Berry, Winter, Steeleye and The Crows to name a handful — but David Bowie has stuff going for him that most people haven't even thought of yet. And he's got nice legs, too."

A review of the Rainbow concert was printed in *Plays And Players* in the November of 1972; "Judy Garland hasn't left us! Re-materialised, reincarnated, her spirit today enjoys a cosmic existence within the inner consciousness of one celestial transvestite poseur, namely David Bowie, who

David Bowie - *The Rise And Fall Of Ziggy Stardust*

recently returned to Earth with something like the impact of nuclear fission. In a solid two-hour performance at the London rock venue ironically called the Rainbow, David demonstrated in an explosive manner just what it's all about. I expected rock; most of the audience probably expected rock. The main course however was theatre — living theatre. Synthesised strains of Beethoven from *A Clockwork Orange* set the scene as, amid a mist of dry ice, David pranced on stage, complete with makeup and sparking astral outfit, to render 'Lady Stardust'. The Spiders — the name the trio of Mick Ronson, Trevor Bolder and Woody Woodmansey appear to have acquired as a result of the success of *The Rise And Fall Of Ziggy Stardust And The Spiders From Mars* — joined him, and above, The Astronettes appeared one by one. The Astronettes are an extraordinary group of mime artists, led by mime expert Lindsay Kemp, whose routines David has made an integral part of the music."

"*Ziggy Stardust* formed the core around which everything was built. The LP, aside from its musical merits or demerits, contains an extremely sophisticated "rock story" — not sophisticated so much in terms of its theme as in the way that theme is put across, with David using varying levels of involvement, from total detachment to absolute identification with the main character, to convey his idea: that of the rise and fall of a superstar. Unlike Christ, possibly the first superstar, Ziggy Stardust is to be one of the last, for there are only five years left to cry in — Earth is dying. Hence the connection with *A Clockwork Orange* (which has obviously become a "now" cult with Beethoven's remains no doubt doing their best to writhe as audiences clap along to the beat of the glorious Ninth); the world of Ziggy Stardust has similarities with that of Alex and his Droogs. Similarities too with *Cabaret*, and its implications: the glamour, the sexual ambiguity, the decadence, it's all there — only now Joel Grey has moved from MC to superstar."

Live Performances

"The Ziggy story was not laboriously retold, however. The makeup, the costumes, the mime and such provided background whilst songs like 'Five Years', 'Starman', 'Lady Stardust' and 'Suffragette City' implied the basic theme. This structure was completed with material from two of David's other albums. *The Man Who Sold The World* is an earlier LP just being "discovered" by the public, but deemed his greatest musical achievement so far by some critics. As well as a couple of longer numbers from this, there were several from the more recent *Hunky Dory*, including the last single 'Changes', David's tribute to Andy Warhol, and one of my favourites, 'Queen Bitch'. But back to Miss Garland; the entire evening seemed like a tribute to Judy. David Bowie, his delicate face made-up to look like hers, has the guts, the glitter, the charm, the force, the remoteness — the star qualities — of Garland and, yes, even the legs. During one of his numbers, he disappeared from the stage for a few moments and returned, having shed his stardust suit, sporting a multi-coloured leotard and a shapely pair of legs. And that after he'd worked the title line from 'Over The Rainbow' into a verse of 'Starman'! The audience responded just as they might have done, ten or twenty years ago to Judy, riotously applauding at the beginning of, end of, and in some cases (such as 'Space Oddity', which had been reworked to allow audience "participation" in the blast off) in the middle of the numbers."

"The set made that of *Jesus Christ Superstar* look like the stage for a school play, and David was around for a couple of nights, not for a long running West End musical. The multi-layered design included platforms at either side with ladders stretching up to them, and mechanically operated backdrop screens, used in conjunction with projectors (film and slide) and an intricately calculated light show. As David and the trio performed their music, The Astronettes danced advanced mime routines, periodically joined by David himself. The biggest difficulty for all concerned was getting into the correct position for the lighting effects at the correct time, but the dancing was mostly quite smooth and sophisticated, although David's movements flowed rather less than the others and occasionally seemed a little shaky."

"David Bowie has been through many changes, resulting in deep and sincere interests in Buddhism and the ancient art of mime, which date back to pre-Space Oddity times. He was responsible for forming the Beckenham Arts Lab, in which he was free to concentrate on Chinese derived movement and help develop mixed media work, and he once appeared at the Royal Festival Hall as a mime artist performing a Tibetan story. The movement of The Astronettes owes much to the Chinese art — swift, dramatic, to the point. One of their routines, which made greatest use of the ladders, had first David and then the rest of the team nimbly running partway up the ladders, then, as if suddenly losing their nerve, gliding back down to the centre of the stage, like scared mice who are afraid to venture too far from their hole."

"Two hours is a long time, both for artists and audience, and by the end both seemed exhausted. David must certainly have stamina — to dance and sing like that for so long where many more conventional performers would have relied on pre-recorded music — and it must have rubbed off on the audience, because they could easily have been staggered by the spectacle. It was a lot to take all in one go, slightly over the top, but one factor held it together more than any: David's voice. This has matured tremendously and now has a clear, liquid quality about it which together with his attractive melancholy tremble, is quite compelling. David is well on the way to achieving the recognition that's been wasted on mortals in recent years. He's on his own, but only because he's different — he has the mystique of a star. The trouble is where next? Traditionally it should be the automobile accident or the overdose, but then he's hardly a traditionalist. Ziggy commits rock 'n' roll suicide.

Live Performances

Maybe he's to suffer the fate of Major Tom in 'Oddity': to float alone in space for eternity."

The 20th October 1972 saw Bowie and The Spiders perform at the Santa Monica Civic Auditorium in Los Angeles. It was a vital performance in terms of how it enabled Bowie to get through to the American market in a big way. For years, the audio of the concert was only available as a bootleg. It wasn't until 1994 that it was given an official release.

The first US Ziggy Stardust tour had kicked off on 22nd September 1972 in Cleveland. Such was the success of the Cleveland show that more dates were added to the tour by demand. Although Bowie wasn't well-known in the US at this time, his star persona and the spread of the word about his amazing stage shows did wonders for his image overall. The US Ziggy Stardust tour was initially only supposed to last until 20th October but the tour was extended for another six weeks. Manager Tony Defries was a pivotal instigator in this. He and Bowie made an ambitious team.

By 16th October 1972, the Bowie entourage was to the strength to nearly fifty people. Arriving in Los Angeles four days before the gig, they stayed in an upmarket Beverly Hills hotel set across twelve acres. The final hotel bill would go on to cost RCA over $100,000 — and a fifth of that was just on room service! Luxurious, the hotel was seen as the place to be; it all helped to boost the enigma of Bowie and his star persona. (On balance though, a lot of money went into more general promotions too. The Ziggy Stardust character featured on promotional material such as skin transfer tattoos).

It was reported in *Rolling Stone* in November 1972; "Today, people involved with Bowie will tell you that he represents the new rock of the seventies and that his American tour is an example of the business style of this new rock. The substance of his business arrangement is a deal between Defries and RCA whereby the record company agreed to underwrite the tour by

David Bowie - *The Rise And Fall Of Ziggy Stardust*

means of a low-interest loan. Record promotion would help stir up concert audiences, and the shows in turn would sell records. RCA figured that even if it lost money on the tour (which, as it turned out, it probably didn't), it would still be worth it. Otherwise, the trick was to treat Bowie as a star even if nobody knew he was yet. Defries, like many managers, refers to both an artist and his music as the "product"." Defries was quoted; "I think making America listen to Bowie in terms of listening to the product and making them aware of the product before he came here, is one way of doing it. The other way is to bring him here without anyone knowing anything about him, and putting him on a second bill, and letting them learn about him firsthand in sleazy, dingy little places for two or three years. I don't think that necessarily is the right way."

Two shows took place at the Santa Monica Civic Auditorium. When the show set for the 20th had sold out quickly, another was promptly booked for the 21st. Given the job of promoting the show was Jim Rismiller, a well-known promoter of shows in that part of the world at the time. Rismiller hadn't heard of David Bowie initially. It was Tony Defries who had keenly informed him.

The Santa Monica Civic Auditorium concert was the first of Bowie's to be broadcast live on American radio. Despite the pressure that Bowie and The Spiders may have been under to deliver a strong performance, they aced it — just as well considering that the auditorium alone could seat 3,000 people and that the radio output could have potentially reached tens of thousands of people. As part of this, the audio of the show became in demand as a bootleg.

On an original FM radio broadcast of the performance, the D.J. enthused; "It's a cool night in Los Angeles and as you may know or not know, the Santa Monica Civic is about a hundred yards from the beach so we have a cool breeze blowing off the ocean through the stage at our backs. The auditorium is packed,

Live Performances

as a matter of fact, for the first David Bowie concert in the Los Angeles area. There will be one more tomorrow night. This is the concert tonight which will be recorded by RCA for the next David Bowie album and we expect to hear some new material by this British superstar. David and his group, The Spiders From Mars, will enter from the other side of the stage. The auditorium is completely blacked out except for flashing strobe lights. Now the entrance music will be the Ode, or should I say the 'Ode To Joy' which is featured in the movie *Clockwork Orange*. And the house lights are starting to dim."

RCA had actually made their own recording of the show. The plan was to release it as a live album in time for Christmas. It was to form part of a double LP along with the material that RCA had already recorded at the Boston Music Hall nearly three weeks prior.

It's fortunate that some rather interesting variables were not visible to the majority of people who got to hear the concert. Mick Ronson was suffering from sunburn as a result of having enjoyed his time relaxing by the outdoor pool in the hotel a little too much. Not only that, but Bowie's hairdresser (Ronson's future wife) Sue Fussey, had to bleach his hair back to blond; it had gone green as a result of swimming in the chlorinated pool! Bowie on the other hand, was pale. He had spent a lot of his time at the hotel indoors.

In October 1972, the performance was reviewed in the *Los Angeles Times*; "To anyone who had heard his *Hunky Dory* and *Ziggy Stardust* albums, there was little doubt that England's David Bowie was going to be a major figure in rock. As a singer, songwriter and arranger, there was such a consistent quality and vision to those albums that he clearly was a valuable and rewarding artist. In his concerts Friday and Saturday nights at the Santa Monica Civic Auditorium, Bowie, now making his first US tour, confirmed everything those albums suggested. He is a certified, genuine, guaranteed, blue-ribbon star. The

David Bowie - *The Rise And Fall Of Ziggy Stardust*

anticipation level for Bowie was so high Friday night that there were numerous audible shouts for him when the guitarist for the opening act (Sailcat) stepped forward to introduce his group's next number. Twice, the yells for Bowie were so impossible to ignore, the guitarist felt it necessary (or at least wise) to acknowledge them, once by dedicating a song to Bowie and then by assuring the audience that Bowie would be out soon."

"Bowie's arrival on stage was accompanied by a marvellously designed slice of rock drama. The flashing strobe lights and strains of Beethoven's 'Ode To Joy' combined perfectly with the band's futuristic spacesuits and Bowie's own bisexual image to provide an aura of *Clockwork Orange*, not so much in the sense of violence as in an incredible sense of "nowness" and the wave of the future. Future shock had arrived. Bowie, his face covered by a modest layer of white makeup and his carrot-tinted hair so colourful that it looked almost aflame, opened with 'Hang On To Yourself', a song from *Ziggy Stardust* that is a perfect invitation to a rock concert: 'So come on, come on, we've really got a good thing going...'. Two things were immediately apparent. First, Bowie, with a background in mime, has enormous stage control and is able to accomplish more with the mere movement of his eyes than most performers in rock can do with a whole series of exaggerated movements. His body is so disciplined that Bowie can create the tension of a wild animal, a tiger or panther, as he prowls the stage, controlling the pace and direction of the show as he moves."

"Second, the band is a tight and controlled group, one that is able to work as a unit rather than, as with so many bands, a collection of individuals. It can provide all the vigour that a rocker such as 'Suffragette City' requires, yet also offer the fluidity that a song such as 'Changes' demands. Bowie's arrival and opening number are so powerful in their impact that they — particularly when coupled with the flamboyance of the photos that preceded Bowie here in ads and elsewhere — lead

Live Performances

the audience to believe there is going to be more in the area of theatrical dynamics than Bowie actually delivers, causing the audience to re-adjust its expectations."

"Though the Friday audience seemed to accept Bowie's movement from rock to soft to rock again, portions of the Saturday audience — seemingly less culty — exhibited an occasional impatience with the soft numbers. There was some noticeable audience conversation during 'My Death' for instance, and some shouts of 'rock 'n' roll' and other 'get it on' urgings after that song. It isn't, one senses, that Bowie couldn't put together an evening built solely around powerhouse rock rather than divide his time between soft and rock numbers. But that doesn't seem to be his style, it doesn't seem to be his goal. He wants to establish his own unique musical and emotional identity. He doesn't want to be simply a rock 'n' roll star."

"There have been some who have suggested Bowie has the talent, originality and charisma to become some sort of Elvis Presley of the seventies, but his more likely target/model if he had the power to choose a role, would be a sort of male Judy Garland of the seventies. Indeed, his most electric moment, aside from the opening both nights, was when he established the same delicate, separate sense of communication with the audience that reminds you of a Garland. In his most intense and perhaps open portrayal of the evening, he assured the audience (in his 'Rock 'n' Roll Suicide' encore) 'You're not alone... gimme your hands'. And the hands reached up for him. Bowie, there's no doubt about it, is a major star, both in a commercial and most importantly, an artistic sense."

Another key date on the first US leg of the Ziggy Stardust tour was the performance at New York's Carnegie Hall on 28th September 1972. The Beatles had previously performed two concerts there in February 1964 (and never again).

Still a relatively unknown act in the US at the time, it was vital for Bowie to impress an audience in New York. The

David Bowie - *The Rise And Fall Of Ziggy Stardust*

performance was heavily promoted, with even the cast of Andy Warhol's play, *Pork*, recruited to distribute tickets.

As it happened, the concert quickly became the event to be seen at. Tickets sold out quickly and Warhol himself was only able to get hold of just two tickets. Apparently, it was even the case that Ahmet Ertegun (a diplomat's son and President of Atlantic Records) couldn't get hold of a ticket.

A large spotlight was positioned outside of the hall on the night of the performance. It created the aesthetic of an event not to be missed. "Fall in love with David Bowie," said the words put up on the Carnegie Hall marquee. The sights and sounds of just everything outside of the hall attracted hundreds of people who were keen to take in the scene. Many were desperate to grab hold of a last-minute ticket. The demand resulted in tickets initially purchased for $6 being sold for between $30 and $50.

The press turnout for the event was huge. There was someone present from each and every one of the UK music papers. RCA recorded that of the one hundred press passes that they handed out, they had received four hundred requests. Not only that, but a star-studded entourage was present: Andy Warhol, the New York Dolls, Todd Rundgren, Truman Capote, Tony Perkins, Alan Bates, and Jackie Kennedy's sister, Lee Radziwill.

It was argued by some that the entire thing was a publicity stunt, especially in view of the fact that whilst the majority of other performances of the tour made a good profit, the Carnegie Hall date didn't make one at all due to how so many of the tickets had been given away to those who were seen by RCA as desirable to have in attendance.

The pressure was on for Bowie. Prior to his performance, he and some of his entourage had caught a flu virus that was doing the rounds. Although the concert was a success, the way that the illness had an influence on Bowie did not go unnoticed. It was noted in *Rolling Stone* that after his performance at Carnegie Hall, Bowie's "flu had progressed to its stupefaction

Live Performances

stage" and that he "responded to questions in the flu sufferer's manner, with a blank stare into space for about the time it takes to ride a bicycle up a long hill, followed by a fretful harvest of words." Understandably, there was no party after the show. Bowie went back to bed at the Plaza Hotel to recover.

In October 1972, *Billboard* reported on the Carnegie Hall performance; "Ziggy is a myth and Lady Stardust is a song. They are not David Bowie, though each is a part of the other. Bowie set himself a number of impossible requirements for the full success of this tour, and then, being Bowie, proceeded to meet them all with grace. Hard rock volume and violence does not normally allow for the demands of complex lyrics. But Bowie made every line of every song accessible and clear, which is what can happen when you get a former actor turned into a pop star. To live up to a reputation as a colossal showman, he had to have a master's grasp of theatrics. But his controlled movements and gestures on a stark, bare stage only complemented the music, which is what can happen when you get a former mime turned into a pop star. The image, the high camp and the low laughs of the Bowie-lore that preceded him, that's what could have been the music's undoing. But a ghastly pallor, flaming red hair, and a change of clothes from harlequin to high-collared spangle, was all of the image he chose to give. Bowie the performer is serious about his songs. For material, he reached as far back as his two Mercury albums, as far forward as the recent two on RCA, and as far away as Jacques Brel and the Velvet Underground. There were even a few acoustic numbers, with moments for the grand delicacy of the Bowie twelve-string guitar. And in around the practiced gleam of madness and stardom, there was a hint that the performer rather liked being received like a hero. All with good cause. There is less that's impossible now that Bowie's been and gone."

The New York Times reviewed the performance; "Tinselled English rock superstars have been sprouting eagerly all over

David Bowie - *The Rise And Fall Of Ziggy Stardust*

the place this season, but most, unfortunately, have looked as appealing as out-of-date Christmas trees. On Thursday night at Carnegie Hall, David Bowie, one of the most heralded — and, to American audiences, one of the most unknown — of the new theatrical rock stars proved that the whole trend hasn't been a publicity agent's fantasy. The mother country still has a few worthwhile exports for her erstwhile colony. Advance stories about Bowie had most of us expecting a performance that would be little more than a transvestic fashion show with musical accompaniment. But despite Bowie's obvious interest in unusual costuming, makeup and dyed hair, he is a solidly competent stage performer who brings a strong sense of professionalism to every move he makes. Those members of the audience — and there obviously were many — who expected a racier show received a major disappointment. There can be no denying the outright colourfulness of Bowie and his group. He and his band members have dyed their hair various shades, from Bowie's flaming orange to the drummer's snow white. Their costumes, made of a shiny satin-like texture, with tight trousers tucked into laced-up boots, combined with the strangely hued hair and highlighted facial makeup to give the musicians an otherworldly appearance, almost as though they were acting out Bowie's fascination with science fiction. The music is not very familiar, aside from a few tunes — the stuttering 'Changes' is one — that has received some radio play in this country. Unfamiliar or not, it is good music with a sense of sectionalisation and variation that has been woefully rare in much rock music lately. Bowie still doesn't seem to know how to write an appealing melody, but this promise of his talent is crystal clear. Most important, as a performer, Bowie delivered. He understands that theatricality has more to do with presence than with gimmickry, and that beautifully co-ordinated physical movements and well-planned music can reach an audience a lot quicker than aimless prancing and high-decibel electronics.

Live Performances

In an age of publicity overkill, that alone has to be counted a major accomplishment."

In the same month, it was reviewed in *Record World*; "Even Andy couldn't get a third ticket; David Bowie's first concert in New York at Carnegie Hall was the toughest ticket in town, in the Event class with Elvis and the Stones. From hard rocking kids to executives that had yet to be convinced of their own hype, the Apple's boogaloo dudes sat amazed while Bowie proved once and for all that his act, his songs, his style were all one needed to know about the Face of 1972, whose photos most of us know so much better than his music. A few were disappointed; they had expected Alice Cooper, Iggy Pop, Jim Morrison, and Mick Jagger, all in drag, and what they got was an intimate, tasteful, and dignified young man, whose performance seemed closer to Marlene Dietrich or Edith Piaf than the late lamented Ziggy Stardust. In fact, tunes from Bowie's latest RCA album, *The Rise And Fall Of Ziggy Stardust And The Spiders From Mars*, seemed to fall into clear perspective for the first time, as Bowie combined them with earlier masterpieces like 'Space Oddity' and 'Width Of A Circle'. They did what Bowie's agent calls the 'rock and roll show' to distinguish it from the theatre extravaganza, with pantomimists and dancers, which David mounted at London's Rainbow Theatre shortly before he embarked on his first American tour. It is a surprisingly straight-forward set, despite the difficulty of some of the material. After one gets over the initial impression of the band's highly styled, reptile-tight futuristic costumes, guitarist Mick Ronson's platinum blond super-image, and the remarkable dexterity of drummer Woody Woodmansey and bassist Trevor Bolder, it is David's face and hands and voice that captivate and focus attention on the flow, beat, and content of the incomparable songs. He appears then not as a gay boy, a transvestite, a theatrical rocker, or a Bolanish hype, but as an artist who even without force or flash

David Bowie - *The Rise And Fall Of Ziggy Stardust*

compels hushed respect. New York audiences are not generally renowned for hushed respect."

"Bowie began with his current theme song 'Hang On To Yourself', but quickly moved on to a variety of material from his last four albums. The show is beautifully paced, mixing up such poles of Bowie's genius as 'Life On Mars' and 'Suffragette City', 'Starman' and 'Andy Warhol' ('for all the blonds in the audience') with no sense of strain or pretension. The band is the sharpest, tightest and tastiest trio since the original Beck group, sans Nicky Hopkins and Rod Stewart. They could be a hot band on their own, but it is greatly to Bowie's credit that he turns them on enough for them to add new dimensions to his older songs as they perform them today. Previously, they had used Cream's 'I Feel Free' to knock the audience over with their virtuosity, not coincidentally allowing Bowie time to slip offstage and change outfits. Now the extended bizarre personal odyssey 'Width Of A Circle' is the vehicle, and like The Who's medley from *Tommy* or the Stones' live version of 'Midnight Rambler', it is hard to believe a show can go on from there. But Bowie had some Lou Reed to get across, so 'like bringing coals to Newcastle', he lit into 'Waiting For The Man' and 'White Heat', driving those songs harder than the Velvets, who lived them, ever could. When the audience stood and laughed, whistled, stomped and generated for David, who had in a short hour and a half become a rocking reality the like of which we just don't hear anymore, there was nothing left to do but boogie on with 'Round And Round'. A smile, a sincere 'thank you', and away. People have been talking about David Bowie for years, and even now that he is here and turning his cult into a superstar's following, there are those who will write him off as a hype, because they can't cope with the energy, the confusion, the politics, and perhaps their disappointment because tickets were scarce and nobody was petted into self-importance for liking David Bowie. Bowie's show is his own best justification; no more needs be said, and

Live Performances

eventually as with Alice and Jagger, words will be superfluous. For the time being, we should note that David Bowie sold 4,300 seats in Memphis on a Sunday night, that his 'All The Young Dudes' as performed by Mott The Hoople is bulleting up the charts, and that *Ziggy Stardust* is one of the year's biggest albums in Britain. David Bowie is the cat's P.J.s."

It was considered in *Melody Maker*; "A sense of boredom was beginning to hang over New York. The streets don't buzz anymore. Neither do the nights. Everyone is sensing it. And when David Bowie arrived the reason became obvious — American rock 'n' roll is still hanging onto the sixties. It's rather like watching an old horse clatter onwards. No matter how many new riders you put on it, the horse doesn't get any younger. Bowie arrived on a sleek, silver machine, pushing that old horse into the gutter, and covering it with dust. The nag will be allowed to get up again, because American record companies are dead as dog's meat. It won't last much longer though. It can't."

Two weeks earlier, Bowie had arrived on the QE2, and nested with his entourage at the ultra-sharp Plaza Hotel. It was viewed as a mild but worrying invasion by some. A collection of people with short-cropped hair and white faces were to be seen in the city the following night. To an extent, the States regarded Bowie as a manufactured star because previously, he wasn't well known there. Eight dates were scheduled for a two month stay — hardly a workingman's tour. They stayed in the best hotels and were guarded from doing too many interviews. It generated hype. The mystery and excitement grew, thus proving it to be a wise move. As previously mentioned, rumour had it that RCA had bought up nigh on half of the tickets for the Carnegie date. It was one that RCA themselves would not completely deny.

Bowie struck it lucky with his Carnegie Hall concert; not much else was going on in the city that week. Much interest

David Bowie - *The Rise And Fall Of Ziggy Stardust*

surrounded the date. The cloak of mystery had worked. There was a searchlight planted outside the hall. It spun around slowly in a circle, abundantly commanding attention. Many people stood outside, jostling for spare tickets. It was Bowie's first concert in New York, and there were already touts about.

As *Melody Maker* reported, "Can't be bad. I've never seen quite such a strange gathering of people that nattered, and posed around the Carnegie Cafe to the left, and downstairs in the hall. For a start, there were many people who resembled Christmas trees on legs. There was much glitter, and several men dressed as ladies. As somebody quite rightly said, 'The sixties are over, well and truly over.' The quiver of excitement that ran up the legs of the audience just before 9pm was extraordinary. It was really excitement. You could feel it, and if you shut your eyes, and thought very hard — you could touch it — an electrical thing that crackled in the air. A strobe was turned on, and the familiar tones of *Clockwork Orange* music cut the air, very loud, and quite suddenly there was Bowie in New York City. A figure seen to be plugging in a twelve-string jumbo. A figure that was continually falling to pieces, as the strobes played their tricks. How lovely it all was — a rock 'n' roll band kicking up dirt and attacking. Bowie was trying every minute and working like fury. And glory did it work. Mick Ronson was playing rock guitar like it should be played. No frills, just a quick wrist. The audience just loved him."

"The first ten minutes were great, then it all fell a little with a couple of numbers that appeared to have too many ingredients. Wide-eyed Bowie was sensing everything mind, and he kicked it all back up, and then cooled it completely by sitting on a stool and chunking out 'Space Oddity'. What a lovely song that is. Bowie announced that he'd picked up a forty-eight-hour virus, but he was still sizzling with energy, singing like a wild thing in that lean, cultured voice. He was something to watch, something to get off to. Half-way through

Live Performances

he'd captured the audience. There wasn't an ounce of laziness about, Bowie was out to entertain. There was a really fat old chap who sat three seats away — a reporter from a really fat old newspaper. He was taking notes by the dozen and had a puzzled look across his face. Bowie had a smile from ear to ear when he delivered the Warhol ditty, and then announced that he was 'kind of bringing coals to Newcastle with two Velvet underground numbers'. They fairly stomped along and a piece of the audience got up, and started dancing. 'Waiting For The Man' was just crazy — one might confidently say he's added much to that number. Then 'White Light' and the Carnegie ran spare with fun. What a fun evening it was. A standing ovation, it had to be. And such a constant roar for an encore that he came back and did Chuck's 'Round And Round'. Even when he delivered that, his face didn't wander from the one expression it had kept all evening. It was an almost child-like, innocent, smiling face, filled with imagination and bright eyes. He seemed to know all the time that it would work."

Billboard reported in November 1972; "RCA artist David Bowie continues to add more concerts to his first US tour. The UK singer has added a second show at a 10,000 seater venue in Cleveland for 26th November. His first Cleveland concert — a sellout — is on 25th November. In Philadelphia, two shows have been added to initial booking... Additionally there is a boom in Bowie album product. Two albums, previously released on Mercury but picked up in a master deal by RCA, entered the *Billboard* album chart this week — *Space Oddity* at 136 and *The Man Who Sold The World* at 170. Bowie's *The Rise And Fall Of Ziggy Stardust* album is currently in the *Billboard* listing at ninety seven after twenty three weeks."

On 3rd July 1973, Bowie performed what he would announce to be his last appearance as Ziggy Stardust. The performance at Hammersmith's Odeon Theatre in London was the last one of the Ziggy Stardust tour.

David Bowie - *The Rise And Fall Of Ziggy Stardust*

By this point, the tour had been going on for nearly a year and there had been little opportunity to take any time off. Tony Defries had been hoping to take the tour to Europe and then to the US once more, so much so that dates had been booked from 1st September 1973 at Toronto's Maple Leaf up to and including 31st October at San Antonio in Texas. There had even been talk between Bowie and Defries about the scope of extending the tour into 1974 with dates in China and the USSR. Despite all of this though, Bowie took matters into his own hands at the Hammersmith Odeon on 3rd July 1973.

Another theory existed at the time that despite Defries' and Bowie's ambitions, it may have been that RCA had forced both of them to retire the tour (or if not forced, certainly influenced). Although Bowie's albums had succeeded to give RCA a return on their investment, it would have been expensive to further the Ziggy Stardust tour to the extent that had been discussed.

The latter aside of course, Bowie had already booked studio time for what would be his next album, *Pin Ups* (the album following *Ziggy Stardust*, *Aladdin Sane*, had been released in April 1973). Besides, as Bowie revealed years later; "I wanted the whole MainMan thing away from me. It was circusy. I was never much of an entourage person — I hated all of that. It's a relief for all these years — not to have a constant stream of people following me around to the point where, when I sat down, fifteen other people sat down. It was unbearable. I think Tony saw himself as a Svengali type, but I think I would have done okay anyway. Now, I look back on it with amusement more than anything else. Everybody was always going to get their teeth done or something, brand new people appearing in the office, having changed their appearance completely from the day before, and so forth."

Inevitably, Bowie's "retirement announcement" at the end of the show came as a shock to the fans. It turned out that prior to making the announcement, Bowie had only told Defries and

Live Performances

Ronson of his plans. It was apparently even news to Angie when David announced it on stage. Although Mick Ronson would go on to be supported by Defries in a solo career, the announcement spelled the end for The Spiders.

The final concert was also unique in that it featured Jeff Beck. He joined everyone on stage to play 'Round And Round' and 'The Jean Genie/Love Me Do' (on which Bowie contributed harmonica).

Jeff Beck was a hero of Ronson's. *Record Collector* considered in 1993; "David Bowie turned the Jeff Beck worshipping Hull guitarist into his sidekick and fellow star, but Ronson proved to have the staying power beyond the lifetime of Ziggy Stardust."

Once Beck had left the stage, Bowie famously announced; "Everybody, this has been one of the greatest tours of our lives. I would like to thank the band, I would like to thank our road crew, I would like to thank our lighting people. Of all of the shows on this tour, this particular show will remain with us the longest because not only is it the last show of the tour, but its the last show that we'll ever do. Thank you."

As shocked fans screamed out in disapproval and disappointment, Bowie's bodyguard protected him from the sea of hands grasping out at him onto the stage. A tape of 'Land Of Hope And Glory' was then played.

Following the 3rd July show, the music and mainstream UK papers ran the story of "Bowie Quits". Little did they know that it was only the Ziggy Stardust persona that Bowie was retiring and as part of that, The Spiders.

The 1980 Floor Show (named as a wordplay on the song, '1984') was to truly be Bowie's last appearance as Ziggy Stardust. It was also to be the last time that Mick Ronson and Trevor Bolder played with Bowie as Spiders. The show was filmed over three days for the American TV show, *The Midnight Special*. Most of the filming took place at London's

David Bowie - *The Rise And Fall Of Ziggy Stardust*

Marquee Club in Soho.

Bowie had been approached to do the show by Burt Sugarman as part of *The Midnight Special*'s rock series. Bowie came up with the idea of doing a full-blown theatrical show with not only himself as Ziggy Stardust, but with several other rock groups. Marianne Faithfull, The Troggs and a Spanish vocal group by the name of Carmen all performed as part of the show. Bowie had full artistic control of the project, as had been agreed in the contract set up by music industry specialist lawyer, Michael Lipman.

When it was announced that the show was to go ahead, several UK newspapers commented about how unjust it was that nothing of the show was going to be broadcast on UK TV.

Despite the amount of footage that was filmed, the final programme consisted of a one-hour show. It was broadcast on America's NBC TV on 16th November 1973. Although the show is still sometimes repeated on American TV, it isn't available as a commercial release.

Everyone in attendance in the audience at the show's filming had been selected exclusively from the recently formed International David Bowie Fan Club. Members of the music press were among the guest list as well as Lionel Bart, Tony Visconti, Mary Hopkins, Dana Gillespie, Long John Baldry and Wayne County. And of course, wife Angie and son, Zowie Bowie.

Correctly, Tony Defries had told *Rolling Stone* in November 1972; "Bowie is setting a standard in rock and roll which other people are going to have to get to if they want to stay around in the seventies. I think he's very much a seventies artist. I think most of the artists who are with us at the moment are sixties artists, and Bowie, certainly to me, is going to be the major artist of the seventies. In 1975, he will be at his peak in music. What he does after that is going to depend on what his talents are in other fields... I want to see him on film. I want to see him making feature films."

Chapter Four
A Legacy

The *Rise And Fall Of Ziggy Stardust And The Spiders From Mars* was a vital album for David Bowie. Not only did it make him a household name, but it made for a live tour that pushed the boundaries of what was expected of a group on stage at the time. With use of theatrics including dance, special effects and changes of elaborate costumes, the performances have remained an iconic part of music history to this day.

With the advantage of hindsight, *Ziggy Stardust* has been categorised as both glam rock and rock opera. Whilst they can be helpful labels, really, the work comes into its own. Especially in terms of how it combined so many original and interesting ideas, both musically and in terms of production and performance. *Rolling Stone* considered in June 1987; "With *The Rise And Fall Of Ziggy Stardust And The Spiders From Mars*, David Bowie created not only his most colourful public persona but also one of his most enduring musical efforts. 'I packaged a totally credible plastic rock star,' Bowie said of the Ziggy character, a doomed messianic rocker who sported futuristic costumes, heavy makeup and close-cut orange hair. The *Ziggy* album (featuring such Bowie classics as 'Starman', 'Soul Love', and 'Suffragette City') and the stunningly theatrical stage shows that Bowie and his crack band put on to promote it were central to the rise of "glam" rock. Of the sound he helped create, Bowie said recently, 'It seems to have permeated every area of rock now'."

David Bowie - *The Rise And Fall Of Ziggy Stardust*

Vitally, *Ziggy Stardust* was essential in securing the interest of an American audience. It had been keenly anticipated there and then given positive reviews as Bowie's profile increased with touring. With photos of the album's artwork, *Billboard* urged on their front cover feature in June 1972; "David Bowie packs a cosmic clout on his newly-released album, titled, resoundingly enough, *The Rise And Fall Of Ziggy Stardust And The Spiders From Mars*. The British rock-and-roller gets down to that old galactic boogie like it's never been gotten down to before. The equally stellar single is 'Starman'."

Record World reviewed the album in May 1972; "This will be the one that does it for the incredible Mr Bowie. His best effort to date, and commercial in every sense. For those easily frightened, just listen. It's great."

Cash Box reviewed it in the same month; "If they are still putting phonograph records in time capsules, then we would like to recommend the new Bowie for inclusion. David's latest full-scale invasion of the mind is the telling saga of a rock and roll star's trek through a garden of unearthly delights. The songs are uniformly brilliant and the production by Bowie and Ken Scott is virtually flawless. It's an electric age nightmare. It's a cold hard beauty. It's another example of the shining genius of David Bowie. An album to take you into the 1980s."

It was reviewed by *Billboard* in the June; "Nineteen and seventy-two may well go down as the year Davy Bowie put the glitter and glamour back into rock. He is almost an indestructibly sensitive lyricist in popdom. Already an avant-garde superstar, this album will make him accessible to the masses for home consumption. His vocal flamboyance scores most obviously on 'Star', 'Suffragette City' and 'Starman'."

In September 1972, *Record World* considered that RCA had been "responsible for breaking perhaps the most important new talent of the year, David Bowie" and that "Bowie had already produced a fine pop album on Deram in 1967 and two more avant-

A Legacy

garde LPs for Mercury in 1969-1970. But aside from his British top five hit single, 'Space Oddity', the very personification of glamour for the seventies had yet to break very largely in even his native England. After receiving stupendous notices for his very perceptive as well as commercially charming *Hunky Dory*, his debut disc on RCA, Bowie tore England up as his next LP, *The Rise And Fall Of Ziggy Stardust And The Spiders From Mars*, with its companion single 'Starman', raced up the British charts and stayed there. Bowie is on the verge of his first major American tour, set for next month, and his name and/or picture appear weekly on the covers of such widely-read British music mags as *Melody Maker* and *Disc*. A versatile artist, Bowie is producing Lou Reed's second solo album for RCA in England and has produced and written a top five single for rockers Mott The Hoople."

In January 1981, the *Ziggy Stardust* album made a return to the UK chart where it peaked at number seventy-three. Following this, the *Aladdin Sane* album was reissued. Met with a positive reception, it spent twenty-four weeks on the chart. The renewed interest was based on not only the emerging trend of the New Romantic era, but the success of Bowie's 1980 hit, 'Ashes To Ashes'. Following Bowie's death from cancer on 10th January 2016, *Ziggy Stardust* once again made a dent in the US charts, only this time, it reached a new peak of number twenty-one on the US *Billboard* 200. To date, it is estimated that over 7.5 million copies of *Ziggy Stardust* have been sold worldwide.

Of course, by the early eighties, the nostalgia for *Ziggy Stardust* and the admiration for Bowie's performance remained strong. In 1983, *Record Mirror* reviewed *Ziggy Stardust: The Motion Picture*; "This film, for all its faults, shows Bowie truly as a product of his time. The audience have Oxford bags, long, limp hair with middle partings, turquoise eye shadow, tank tops. And in the middle of all this absurdity slinks and stomps Ziggy

David Bowie - *The Rise And Fall Of Ziggy Stardust*

Stardust — larger than life, towering on grotesque platform shoes, contorting his anorexic frame and pulling all attention towards him with pure magnetism — an over-used word but the only one for this context. Ten years later and a clean and sanitised Bowie is still at the top. With a new record company, his previous business links are exploiting his continued success by the release of both the film and soundtrack. And RCA and former production company MainMan are secure in the knowledge that though the man has gone on to pastures new, he can still bring the money rolling in for them. The result is a strange film. Badly shot in places, with unsubtle attempts to gain laughs at the seated audience's expense, the sense of having caught a piece of history still manages to shine out. To see Ronson, Bolder and Woodmansey again, to hear those guitar solos that somehow never sounded quite as boring as other people's. And then there's the songs. If the Ziggy image was perfect tack, the music was just perfect. The sound is surprisingly strong, the performance energetic and powerful, the lyrics dated but the tunes not. 'Moonage Daydream', 'Suffragette City', 'Let's Spend The Night Together' — over an hour of hearing and seeing what is essentially just a show, but one with one important feature, the actor himself. No one but Bowie could have got away with singing 'Rock 'n' Roll Suicide' while towering on nine-inch red and yellow heels clad in a (snagged) stocking."

The review continued; "It's hard to say if the film captures what it was like to be at Hammersmith Odeon that night or to have belonged to the whole Ziggy era, but it certainly puts all Bowie's work in focus for those who missed it. He had an across-the-board appeal — young, beautiful and wild, everybody's fantasy if only they would let him. From the perfect flame hair to the horrible shoes, the film shows the caricature for what it was — an actor playing on people's subconscious desires. At one time he's cold and distant as Bowie goes through grade one beginner's mime movements, more reminiscent of Rowan Atkinson than Lindsay Kemp. At another, there's complete self-centredness in the ritual play between Bowie and Mick Ronson, seemingly oblivious to the audience and camera while playing up to them totally. Despite the technical defects, what finally spoils the film are the cuts to the "real" Bowie in his dressing room — making up, changing, smoking a cigarette, superficially chatting with Angie. Such scenes are intrusive. They interrupt the magic of the performance, break into the illusion and destroy the fantasy. It wasn't David Bowie the people went to see, but the Ziggy persona, and all that went with it. Bowie has gone through various changes since then, finally resting at the establishment respectability that 'Let's Dance' and recent screen acting has brought. None of them compare with the character and the show of this film — they are totally different people. It's stupid to think that a too-thin, red-haired, sickly-skinned individual with dodgy teeth, disfigured eyes and a fetish for biting his guitarists private parts could result in the most fantastic 'Star' music has produced. The film is sad in a way, because the character's well and truly dead, but as a piece of nostalgia, both for the era and Mr Bowie's earlier life, it's still captivating. The motive for releasing the film may not be the most honourable and it could have been better, but it's all there is. Go along, laugh at the clothes, sing along with the music, and fall in lust all over again."

****

It wasn't long after the first round of success of *Ziggy Stardust* that the directors of K. West took offense to their company name being featured on the album's cover art. So much so that a solicitor for the company issued a statement to RCA: "Our clients are furriers of high repute who deal with a clientele generally far removed from the pop music world. Our clients certainly have no wish to be associated with Mr Bowie or this record as it might be assumed that there was some connection between our client's firm and Mr Bowie, which is certainly not the case."

Fortunately for all concerned, K. West soon became used to and accepting of being a tourist spot. K. West moved out of the Heddon Street location in 1991, taking their sign with them. Bowie said of the sign's removal, "It's such a shame... People read so much into it. They thought "K. West" must be some sort of code for "quest". It took on all these sorts of mystical overtones."

The original sign was removed by a Bowie fan in the early 1980s. So iconic did the location of the photoshoot turn out to be that throughout his life, Bowie would be sent hundreds of photos from fans taken at the same site. It seems that such photos were amongst a range of interesting communications from fans. When asked about what sort of fan mail he received, Bowie said on the *Russell Harty Plus Pop* programme in 1973; "It's very sexy, I seem to draw a lot of fantasies out of people in the fan mail I get. A lot of it is awfully nice, asking 'how's your baby?', 'how's your wife?' and 'what's your mum's name?' but some of them are worth framing."

The appreciation of the *Ziggy Stardust* cover art remained strong. In January 2010, Royal Mail issued it on one of the stamps as part of their Classic Album Cover collection.

In March 2012, owners of Regent Street and Heddon Street, The Crown Estate, installed a commemorative brown plaque — at number twenty-three: in exactly the same place as where the "K. West" sign used to be. The plaque was unveiled by Gary Kemp and the event was attended by Woodmansey and Bolder. The plaque was the first to be installed by The Crown Estate. It is one of the few in the country made in devotion to a fictional character.

****

A Legacy

Ever the creative chameleon, it is clear that Bowie didn't want the Ziggy Stardust character to define him. In an interview with *New Musical Express* in July 1972, Bowie was asked; "What's gonna be the next post-Ziggy development? Have you started to think about a new album?" His response: "No, not at all. I'm still totally involved with Ziggy. I probably will be for a few months getting it entirely out of my system, and then we'll don another mask."

He went on to create a new character by the name of his later album, *Aladdin Sane*. Bowie described the album as "Ziggy goes to America". He said in 1987; "I think I moved out of Ziggy fast enough so as not to be caught by that one. Because most rock characters that one can create only have a short lifespan. They are one shots, they are cartoony. And the Ziggy thing was worth about one or two albums before I couldn't really write anything else around him or the world that I wanted to sort of put together for him."

In April 1973, *New Musical Express* reviewed *Aladdin Sane*; "Bye-bye, Ziggy. It was nice seeing you, and I hope you'll keep in touch. Hello, Aladdin Sane, make yourself at home. David Bowie's new album is just about ready for you, and with it comes a whole new set of hypotheses, poses, masks, games, glimpses, put-ons, take-offs and explored possibilities. More prosaically: one new record, nine David Bowie compositions (two slightly used) and mildly outrageous reworking of 'Let's Spend The Night Together'. Three months ago, I sat on the floor in the mixing room at Trident Studios in the company of David Bowie, Mick Ronson, Ken Scott and sundry others and heard the bulk of this album hot off the tapes. Since then I've carried the memory of it around with me, waiting to hear it again and see how accurately I'd remembered it. Even with that preparation, it's still quite a brainful to assimilate at one hurried mental gulp. In an ideal world, one could give it a fortnight's uninterrupted listening before attempting to tell

David Bowie - *The Rise And Fall Of Ziggy Stardust*

anyone about it, but as you may have noticed if you've been reading the papers, we do not live in anything even vaguely approaching an ideal world. So, for the better or for worse, here are a few snap impressions on my first day with *Aladdin Sane*. Firstly, the cover, which will be a definite asset to any chic home. You'll see it strewn on Axminster carpets in expensive colour supplement stereo ads and carried with token attempts at unobtrusiveness under the arms of the fashionable. On the front is a head and shoulders shot of David with blush-pink make-up and a startling red and blue lightning bolt painted across his face and a small pool of liquid behind one collarbone. Inside, with more lightning bolts, is David nude, but with a silver-grey solarisation that hides the naughty bits. Somewhere in the process he's lost his feet, which was hopefully not too painful."

"So you play the record. Immediately Mick Ronson's guitar roars out of the speakers, and you're sucked straight into 'Watch That Man', a nightmare party sequence straight out of Dylan's 'Ballad Of A Thin Man', where 'There was an old-fashioned band of married men...'. It's a nice, tough opener. With the title song, Bowie sets to in earnest. Its full title is 'Aladdin Sane (1913-1938-197?)'. It will be noted that the first two dates marked the prelude of two world wars, and the third — well, have you checked the papers lately? It's the first real outing for pianist Mike Garson, who spans time and place like most pianists span octaves. Imagine Cecil Taylor playing in a thirties nightclub the day after the atomic catastrophe, and you may have some idea of what Garson lays down. Aladdin, it appears, is going off to fight: 'Passionate bright young things take him away to war,' sings David with a kind of deadpan melancholy, as Ronson's guitar howls like a wolf with its foot caught in a trap and Garson's ornately menacing piano tinkles like the very fabric of existence itself slowly shattering into icy splinters. Would you believe the most unusual anti-war song of all time? Well, that's only track two. As Garson hammers his final chord, we're straight into 'Drive-In Saturday', with which you're probably already familiar. So let's rush headlong into 'Panic In Detroit', which recalls the Stones just a little bit, and the Yardbirds are in there as well, courtesy of Mick Ronson's Beckish guitar. It's a faintly impressionistic tale of a revolutionary group wiped out by the police, and it may refer to the Ann Arbor White Panthers and John Sinclair. The title is endlessly reiterated. Finally for the first side, 'Cracked Actor', which is about an elderly movie star who picks up a young girl, thinking that she wants him for his fame and not realising that she thinks he's her smack connection. The spirit of Lou Reed hangs over this track as David sings: 'Crack baby crack…'."

"The first track on side two is 'Time', intellectually the heaviest thing on the album. Like *Aladdin* itself, it features Garson up front. If *Ziggy Stardust* was David's *Clockwork Orange* album this is his *Cabaret* and the thirties vamp behind the voice makes the lyrics even more sinister than they might otherwise seem. Only David Bowie could sing the words 'We should be on by now' and make them imply that somehow mankind has taken a wrong turning. Not making way for the homo superior perhaps? 'The Prettiest Star' was written three years ago and issued as the follow-up single to 'Space Oddity' on Mercury, but it was deleted and never issued on an album. Here, it's been re-recorded. It's a light little song dedicated to Angie and serves as a wind-down period after the intensity of 'Time'. Hot on its heels is David's own reading of Mick and Keith's 'Let's Spend The Night Together', as premiered at the Rainbow, with Garson playing the riff in augmented chords and David doing an Eno on Moog. It rips and snorts just like it ought to, and then we're into 'Jean Genie' revisited before the closer 'Lady Grinning Soul', which shows that even when David's sentimental, he's doing it in style. The above notes are first impressions. The album's changed slightly since I first heard the tapes in that the recut 'John, I'm Only Dancing' has

David Bowie - *The Rise And Fall Of Ziggy Stardust*

been replaced by 'Let's Spend The Night Together', originally intended as the B-side of 'Drive-In Saturday', and a then incomplete track called 'Zion' has been replaced by 'Lady Grinning Soul'. After some more concentrated listening, some different things might emerge, and in that event I'll take some space later to discuss them. Meanwhile, how does it stack up against its predecessors? I don't know. David Bowie's last three albums have become so deeply embedded in my head that it takes considerable effort to integrate a successor into that patch of brain cells that store his music. One thing I know is that *Aladdin Sane* is probably the album of the year, and a worthy contribution to the most important body of musical work produced in this decade."

Aladdin Sane was also reviewed in *Melody Maker* in the same month; "Oh, he's good all right. Image-wise, he carries it all off with a dazzling, effortless sense of style which makes every other band in the glam/glitter/outrage/theatre-rock field look like something out of a Camping For Beginners. And musically, he and Mick Ronson and Mick Woodmansey and Trevor Bolder and the rest are light-years ahead in their cruel precision. But how deep does it go? Is David Bowie really saying anything much at all? As Ziggy Stardust, rock and roller, he gets it on, no doubt about it. But judged against the standards of the astral image which he and his followers have nurtured — the whole Starman, *Stranger In A Strange Land* aura — his achievements have been disappointing. This was brought home forcibly the other week by Bowie's appearance on the Russell Harty TV show. While he was singing he was perfect: the whole scintillating bisexual image, guaranteed to throw the entire population of straight Britain into panic. And musically, he and the band were machine-tooled perfection. But as soon as he sat down to talk, the whole image dissolved like runny mascara. What he had to say was in no way futuristic, or profound, or controversial. He was as The Prettiest Starlet. It's

A Legacy

not that I expect profundity from a rock star. But when your songs deal in cosmic concepts you are inviting judgement at a pretty high level. And the sad truth is that five minutes of a film like *2001* or one chapter of Asimov or Clarke says more about what man can or will become than the entire body of Bowie's "futuristic" songs."

"It's the same story with this latest album, which is superficially stunning and ultimately frustrating. The title is a pun, of course, and a deadly accurate one. The lyrics are more intense, more strung-out, more fragmented than anything he's done before: splintered nightmare images of a journey across America. At times the lyrics reach that level of obscurity which it is fashionable to describe as "oblique" but which sound to me merely confused and hastily thrown together. Musically, the songs are executed with a brutal panache which puts this album closer to satanic *The Man Who Sold The World* than *Hunky Dory* or *Ziggy Stardust*. Melodically the songs have Bowie's usual flair — 'The Jean Genie' and 'Drive-In Saturday' have already proved themselves as singles and most of the others here are just as catchy, especially 'The Prettiest Star', a very poppy reworking of an old song from 'Space Oddity' days. 'Watch That Man' and 'Panic In Detroit' are stormers with a strong Rolling Stones feel — although Bowie's version of 'Let's Spend The Night Together' is very un-Stonesy, precise and asexual. 'Cracked Actor' is probably the most successful cut: a vividly powerful tale of Hollywood, heroin and sexual cruelty. But the two key works here, I suppose, are the title track and 'Time'. Both have a strained alienated feel, heightened by the fractured jagged piano of new man Mike Garson, but the lyrics promise far more than they actually deliver — which is the way I feel about the whole album. There is much to dazzle the eye and ear, but little to move the mind or heart. It is clever, but icy cold, and I have a feeling that the songs here will not be long remembered. But maybe that's the way Mr Bowie wants it, as

David Bowie - *The Rise And Fall Of Ziggy Stardust*

he makes his plans to go into movies and talks about farewell tours. Perhaps, as Andy Warhol once said, everybody should be famous for just fifteen minutes."

Creem reviewed the album in August 1973; "On 'Drive-In Saturday', a song from the new David Bowie album, a space-age couple flirt and 'try and get it on like once before...'. Elsewhere there is an actual Rolling Stones' song, 'Let's Spend The Night Together', camped up for all its offensive worth. The final spoken finale plea, included just in case you're still listening goes: 'They said our love was no fun...'. This is the cut you'll love to hate 'cause this is the performance Bowie'll never live down. So warped a perspective does it present, one's tempted to say this entire album would better have been left below ground, and David Bowie with it. Not only has the "next Dylan?" overstepped his mark, miscalculated his audience, and revealed himself to be only another nut in the big fruitcake — he has blasphemed the Rolling Stones, for which there is no excuse. Like it or not, one doody this smelly does not necessarily stink up a whole album and *Aladdin Sane* is okay in spite of some other mistakes which indicate Bowie has become a knowing victim of his own hype. *The Tides Of Lust* world of Aladdin Sane is an uneasy truce between the past, present and future. Homo superior has evolved from awesome speculation to drugstore reality. Peopled by a cast of cartoon characters — Aladdin, Buddy, Reverend Alabaster, legendary Lorraine, Jung the foreman and his Astronette mate, The Prettiest Star — the songs make reference in cinematic images to an America where the oceans have dried up, the people's sense of the past is conveyed through video, and Detroit has been swiftly depopulated by war in the street. Sex/romance in its major and minor variations (queer, straight, bio, ono, Orphean, fascist, anarchist, inanimate...) is the primary sign of recognition and the big-chief motif of the record. At a spooky party described in 'Watch That Man', the Lou Reed type you gotta look out for 'talks like a jerk/But he could eat you with a fork and spoon'. On the other coast, an ageing movie queen tells it like it is: 'Smack baby, smack is all that you feel.' And there's the Jean Genie who lives on his back and loves chimney stacks."

"Another twenty-three-inch set-up you can stand to talk about more than you can stand to hear, Bowie's appeal is intellectual (unless you go in for smooth-skinned fellas with no eyebrows — the bushier the better I say) and a lyric sheet or headphones are recommended for proper appreciation of his astute albums (of which this is not one). He continues to write often inspired, fascinating lines, but his music is hit and miss. What with 'Width Of A Circle', 'Changes' and 'Five Years', 'Watch That Man' is the one thing you wouldn't expect this LP's opener to be: a predicable Main Street, readymade. 'Aladdin Sane' features one of Bowie's better, more hummable melodies (there aren't many) but gets left-fielded midway through when an avant-gardy exposition takes its pretty time. 'Drive-In Saturday' suffers from the way Bowie pronounces one word — Buddy — like Alice Cooper, and then is subsequently rescued, irony of ironies, by a Van Morrison scat rave-up. 'Time' is conversely irritating in its mockery, not of some other star, but David himself; it's the kind of burlesque cabaret twirl that might come off better live than it does here. I'd just as soon not find out. 'The Prettiest Star' is yet another booger — a 1970 ode to my alter ego — with a stunning guitar intro by Ronson. These disappointing cuts on *Aladdin Sane* suffer from self-indulgence and self-abuse which in turn seem to have been spurned on by Bowie's own self-imposed isolation, both real (business, media) and imagined (psychic) which in turn has given him a lot of artistic mileage. So what? There's some good stuff too. 'Panic In Detroit' and 'Cracked Actor'... The former song concerns itself with the temporary relationship of Bowie/Aladdin and a gun-totin', truck-driving revolutionary ('He looked a lot like Che Guevara'). That opening clincher is introduced by a low-

David Bowie - *The Rise And Fall Of Ziggy Stardust*

end bomp line from Ronson which is quickly vamped up by 'Gimme Shelter' rhythm and chorus. Chugga chugga! There is fighting in the streets and the police are on the loose. Bowie goes to school one day to find his teacher 'crouching in his overalls', somehow scores a trillion dollars, and returns home to find that his cutie has shot himself, leaving Bowie the gun and a suicide note instead of the autograph he'd requested. It's fairly obvious, subtly put together, and quite mesmerising. 'Cracked Actor' would be great to hear on the AM simply because you never will. Mick Ronson skawks out a massive dizbuster of a riff over Trevor Bolder's gracefully lumbering bass and some quick drumming from Woody Woodmansey while Bowie relates the bitching of an S&M inclined daddy and his Sunset and Vine trick."

"If you turn *Aladdin Sane* over you'll find a couple more goodies, which rescue side two from the disaster of 'Time', 'The Prettiest Star' and 'Together'. 'Jean Genie' may've been insinuating itself for a while now: it came out as a single (in slightly different form) last year. Poor little Greenie is the athlete of the future, a splendidly repulsive being reminiscent of a Samuel R. Declaney creation who 'says he's a beautician and sells you nutrition'. Too long and consciously monotonous, a catchy little number nevertheless. 'Lady Grinning Soul' shows just how far afield Bowie can go and still bring off his brand of sweet-lips. Similar to 'Rock 'n' Roll Suicide' in its concluding affirmation of life, love and the pursuit of happiness, 'Lady' salutes the momentary joys of a good fuck who'll 'beat you down at cool canasta' and then drive away in her Volkswagen to cruise for fresh converts. Bowie soars through the vocal in an oddly convincing manner — affected, effeminate, and mawkish. He's the only guy with the nerve-plus-chops to pull it off. Undeniably, David Bowie has got real problems. A very inconsistent live performer who is much too dependant on his charm to ever really step out with the authority R&R needs to render sophisticated lyrics convincingly, he would better serve his own interests by sticking to the studio where he could concentrate more on the musical end of things, and hopefully continue his fine production work (Iggy Pop, Mott The Hoople). Rumour has it that Bowie and The Spiders are breaking up to go their separate ways in the fall after one more tour. Good. May Mick Ronson prevail. *Aladdin Sane* is a complete letdown after the brilliance of *Ziggy* and more especially *Hunky Dory*. As a one-time short-term fan, I have the distinctly unpleasant feeling that Bowie is indeed guilty of the many charges his fag-baiting slanderers have levelled against him. He is hollow — but it has been his forte in the past to describe that vacancy with some degree of insight and lots of lyrical imagination. This album sacrifices insight for its descriptive purposes while various musical booboos call Bowie's self-seriousness blatantly into question. The art doesn't rise above its implication. A strong breeze could whisk *Sane* away at the shortest notice."

Making their stance clear, *Record World* had reviewed 'The Jean Genie' single in November 1972; "After the heroics of Ziggy Stardust, this brand-new cut comes up short. Bowie, usually a master of melody and dynamics, has used an ancient riff on this more rhythmic number. Disappointing."

Although it had a lot to live up to at the time, retrospectively, *Aladdin Sane* has since been regarded as not only a vital landmark in the glam rock genre but one of the most iconic albums of all time. It has been reissued many times over. In 2012, it was re-mastered in time for its fortieth anniversary.

****

By 1974, although *Aladdin Sane* was acknowledged as a worthwhile album, it could be said that *Ziggy Stardust* was still very much the one in the spotlight. *Record World* considered in the June of that year; "Few would argue the fact that David

David Bowie - *The Rise And Fall Of Ziggy Stardust*

Bowie is one of the most influential figures in the turbulent rock scene of the seventies. But his career began in the mid-sixties with his days as David Jones and The Lower Third, and then as David Bowie and the Buzz, when his first records were largely ignored by a public preconditioned to accept a stereotypical idea of the rock performer. With guitarist Mick Ronson, he assembled the backup group later called The Spiders From Mars and in December 1971, *Hunky Dory* was released under a new recording contract with RCA Records, negotiated by Bowie's manager Tony Defries. The next step was the development of the stage show. Together with The Spiders, Bowie began performing extensively in Britain and the US. His following album, *The Rise And Fall Of Ziggy Stardust And The Spiders From Mars*, charted strongly as Bowie's Ziggy Stardust persona became the first space-rock hero of the seventies. The creation of Ziggy enabled Bowie to bring together coherently his diverse artistic pursuits — visual imagery of costumes, electric nuances of uninhibited choreography, the thematic consistency of his music. In short, a type of theatrical rock presentation never before attempted. Two extended tours rapidly built his cult image into a mass following. Using the power that came with importance, he salvaged the much-loved British band, Mott The Hoople (by writing and producing their first hit single and album 'All The Young Dudes') and worked with Lou Reed (producing Reed's successful *Transformer* album). By the end of 1972, *The Rise And Fall Of Ziggy Stardust* had carried Bowie to critical and public acclaim. As a result, RCA released Bowie's two previous Mercury albums which RCA had purchased at the time Bowie signed with the label: *The Man Who Sold The World* and *Space Oddity*. In January 1973, the title cut of the latter album was released in the US and became one of Bowie's biggest hits. It had been a successful single in England in 1969. Bowie kicked off the first of two 1973 international tours with an SRO

A Legacy

Valentine's Day concert at New York's Radio City Music Hall. In May 1973, RCA released Bowie's *Aladdin Sane* album, a complex work reflecting Bowie's nightmarish vision of the American cities he visited while on tour, further legitimising Bowie's status as one of rock's major innovative poets."

The feature continued; "Beginning in July 1973, Bowie retired to the Château d'Hérouville (Chopin's former residence in the south of France) where he recorded his sixth RCA album, *Pin Ups*, a collection of Bowie's favourite rock tunes from the 1964-67 period in London. After its completion he taped his NBC-TV *Midnight Special* entitled *The 1980 Floor Show*. Conceived and designed by Bowie, the show was shot at the London Marquee Club in Soho where he had performed years earlier with his band, David Jones and The Lower Third. Other projects occupying Bowie during his months away from the concert stage were the production of Lulu's single, 'The Man Who Sold The World', and his assistance on the debut RCA albums of his former lead guitarist Mick Ronson (*Slaughter On 10th Avenue*) and close friend Dana Gillespie (*Weren't Born A Man*). In January 1974, Bowie undertook his most ambitious recording project to date, his conceptual album, *Diamond Dogs* (bulleted at fifty-seven) with sessions taking place at the Olympic Studios in London, as well as in Holland. A single from *Diamond Dogs*, 'Rebel Rebel' (at eighty-seven) is spurring sales further. The release of *Diamond Dogs* will be followed by a summer tour, titled The Year Of Diamond Dogs, which will expand the theme of the album into a visual form for stage. The twenty-five date tour, beginning 14th June at The Forum in Montreal and including Madison Square Garden will be followed this fall by a second, which will take Bowie between fifty and seventy cities. The Year Of The Diamond Dogs is also the first tour in which Bowie will create around him the theatrics of his music. Tony Award-winning lighting designer Jules Fisher, after consultation with Bowie, will show

David Bowie - *The Rise And Fall Of Ziggy Stardust*

his musical diversity, playing guitar, sax, Moog synthesiser and Mellotron. Other musicians on the tour will be Herbie Flowers on bass, Tony Newman on drums, Mike Garson on keyboard. This tour, in conjunction with the album, will show of Bowie's electrifying fusion of total musicality."

Bowie said in 1987; "There was a real feeling of inadequacy in that era. I never really felt like a rock singer or a rock star or whatever. I always felt a little bit out of my element which is a ridiculously highfalutin way of looking at it. Now, from my standpoint, when I look back, I realise that from '72 through to about '76, I was the ultimate rock star. I couldn't have been more rock star."

****

Since its initial release, many of the songs from *Ziggy Stardust* have played major influence to a number of artists. Glen Matlock of the Sex Pistols said years after the success of 'God Save The Queen', that the hit single was inspired by 'Hang On To Yourself': "We got a lot of stuff from The Spiders — that riff in 'God Save The Queen' didn't come from Eddie Cochran, it came from Ronno." (Mick Ronson).

Perhaps one of the most well-known covers of 'Ziggy Stardust' is the one done by Bauhaus. In October 1982, it got to number fifteen in the UK. Other artists who have covered the song include Def Leppard, Hootie And The Blowfish, and Nina Hagen.

'Suffragette City' has since been covered by many artists. Just some of those are Boy George, Frankie Goes To Hollywood, Red Hot Chilli Peppers, and U2. In 1999, the song's title was used by Kate Muir for a novel.

In celebration of his fiftieth birthday, on 8th January 1997, Bowie performed a semi-acoustic version of 'Lady Stardust' featuring Gail Ann Dorsey on bass and vocals. It was broadcast

A Legacy

on BBC radio.

Two months after Bowie's passing, Audi used 'Starman' in an advert broadcast as part of the Super Bowl. At the end of the advert is a tribute to Bowie: "In memory of the Starman."

And of course, the memory of 'Starman' and indeed David Bowie will live on. *The Rise And Fall Of Ziggy Stardust And The Spiders From Mars* was just one of many worthwhile projects achieved throughout an innovative and fruitful career. Importantly though, this particular album of Bowie's made an iconic cultural contribution when it was released in 1972 and indeed, beyond.

Discography

Personnel

Original Album
David Bowie – vocals, acoustic guitar, saxophone, arrangements
Mick Ronson – electric guitar, piano, backing vocals, organ, synthesiser, string arrangements
Trevor Bolder – bass guitar, trumpet
Mick Woodmansey – drums
Rick Wakeman – harpsichord (It Ain't Easy) (uncredited)
Dana Gillespie – backing vocals (It Ain't Easy) (uncredited)

David Bowie – production
Ken Scott – production, audio engineering, mixing engineering
Ray Staff – audio engineering

1990 Rykodisc/EMI
Dr Toby Mountain – re-mastering engineering

1999 Virgin Release
Kevin Cann – design
Peter Mew – re-mastering engineering
Terry Pastor – artwork
Paul Hicks – surround sound
Nigel Reeve – re-mastering engineering

Track Listing

All tracks written by David Bowie, except where noted in brackets.

Side One
Five Years – 4:42
Soul Love – 3:34
Moonage Daydream – 4:40
Starman – 4:10
It Ain't Easy (Ron Davies) – 2:58

Side Two
Lady Stardust – 3:22
Star – 2:47
Hang On To Yourself – 2:40
Ziggy Stardust – 3:13
Suffragette City – 3:25
Rock 'n' Roll Suicide – 2:58

1990 Reissue bonus tracks:
John, I'm Only Dancing (1972 single version, new 1990 remix) – 2:43
Velvet Goldmine (Single B-side from the 1975 RCA rerelease of Space Oddity) – 3:09
Sweet Head – 4:14
Ziggy Stardust (February 1971 demo) – 3:35
Lady Stardust (March 1971 demo) – 3:35

2002 30th Anniversary edition, reissue bonus tracks:
Moonage Daydream (Arnold Corns version) – 3:53
Hang On To Yourself (Arnold Corns version) – 2:54
Lady Stardust (demo) – 3:33
Ziggy Stardust (demo) – 3:38
John, I'm Only Dancing – 2:49
Velvet Goldmine – 3:13
Holy Holy (1971 rerecording) – 2:25
Amsterdam (Jacques Brel, Mort Shuman) – 3:24
The Supermen (Alternate version) – 2:43
Round And Round (Chuck Berry) – 2:43
Sweet Head (take 4) – 4:52
Moonage Daydream (new mix) – 4:47

The online record database *Discogs* lists over 300 versions of the album that have been released worldwide in a multitude of formats. For anyone who wishes to delve into the album to that level, then please consult the database. Throughout the RCA years there were two separate variants available (until about 1986) — the UK version and US versions.

Two tracks differ: 'Starman' was remixed for single release. This single mix was also included on the UK album, rather than the album mix that appeared on the US version.

The other track that differed was 'Suffragette City' — the US version contains a noticeable momentary sound drop-out on one channel, the UK version does not.

The UK album matrix numbers were BGBS 0864 & BGBS 0865.

The US versions had the matrix numbers APRS-6814 9S and APRS-6815.

This discography attempts to catalogue all known UK and US releases along with a select few, unusual variations from elsewhere.

UK Original releases
Originally released 16th June 1972.*
*Both Discogs and 45Worlds list the date as 6th however that was a Tuesday and all UK releases were on Fridays.

RCA Victor SF 8287, LP
RCA Victor – P8S 1932, 8-track cartridge
RCA PK 1932, cassette

Reissues
RCA International INTS 5063, LP, 1980
RCA International INTK 5063, cassette, 1980
RCA BOPIC 3, LP Picture disc, 1984
RCA PD84702, CD 1984
EMI 724385566615, 180gsm LP, 1997
EMI 7243 521 900 0 3, CD, 6th September 1999*
*Enhanced. Issued in a jewel case with cover sticker and sixteen page booklet. Enhanced content includes a slideshow and connects to 'bowieNet' if played on a PC.

Simply Vinyl SVLP 275, LP, 2001
Parlophone DBXL1, 180 Gram LP, 26th February 2016
Parlophone DBZSX 40, LP, 2016

Please note: There was an official red vinyl release in Germany in the 2010s and subsequently multiple coloured vinyl releases that were marketed in the UK in 2014 / 2015. However, these are all counterfeits.

Reissues with bonus tracks
EMI CDP 7944002, CD, 1990
EMI CDP 79 4400 0 CD box set, 1990
EMI TC-EMC 3577, cassette, 1990
EMI 794 400-5, DCC, 11th January 1993

30th Anniversary 2CD edition
EMI 5 39826 2, CD, 8th July 2002

US Original releases
RCA Victor   LSP 4702, LP
RCA Victor LSP-4702, LP*
*Stand-up Display-Sleeve
P8S-1932, 8-track cartridge

PK-1932, cassette
RCA EPPA 4702-C, 7" Reel

Reissues
RCA Victor LSP 4702, LP, 1976
RCA Victor AFL1-4702, LP, 1977
RCA Victor AYL1-3843, 110gram LP, 1980
Mobile Fidelity Sound Lab MFSL 1-064, LP, June 1981
RCA Victor PCD1-4702, CD, 1984
Parlophone 219000-PRL2   CD, 1999*
*Enhanced. Issued in a jewel case with cover sticker and sixteen page booklet. Enhanced content includes a slideshow and connects to 'bowieNet' if played on a PC.

EMI TOCP-70144, cassette, 2007
Virgin DBZS 40, CD, 2012
Parlophone PRL2-791382   CD, 2014
Parlophone RP2-791382   US   2015
Parlophone DBXL1, 180 Gram LP, 26th February 2016

Reissues with bonus tracks
Rykodisc RCD 10134, CD   1990
Rykodisc RCD 90134, CD box set, 1990
Ryko Analogue RACS 0134, cassette, 1990
RACS 0134-2, Club Edition, cassette, 1990
Ryko Analogue RALP 0134-2, 2LP, clear vinyl, 1990
Virgin 72435 39826 2, CD, 16th June 2002

30th Anniversary 2CD edition
Virgin 72435 39826 2, CD, 16th June 2002

Other notable releases from around the world

Spain:
RCA Victor LSP-4702, LP
Cover has title in Spanish: La Ascendencia Y Caida De Ziggy Stardust Y Las Arañas De Marte. Back cover is not full colour but a blue tint.

Germany:
RCA Victor   LSP-4702, LP
Gatefold sleeve. The inner gatefold merely reproduces the standard inner sleeve that was common to other issues.

Greece:
RCA SKL G 20061, LP
The colourisation of the front cover makes the sky a deeper blue. The back cover is monochrome and entirely different; it includes an article from *Rolling Stone* magazine entitled "Bowie's Cosmic Boogie".

Japan:
RCA RCA-6050, LP, 25th October 1972
Includes a four-page insert with liner notes in Japanese and lyrics in English.

Venezuela:
RCA Victor LPVS-1322, LP
Front cover has the words "Napoleon Bravo presenta en Venezuela a:" above Bowie's name. The colourisation is also different and the back cover is monochrome.

Singles

Only 'Starman' was released as a single from the album in 1972. In most countries it was coupled with 'Suffragette City'. In Italy and Spain the B-side was the non-album track 'John, I'm Only Dancing'. In Portugal 'Starman' was released as a 4-track EP with 'Hang Onto Yourself', 'John, I'm Only Dancing' and 'Suffragette City'.

'Rock 'n' Roll Suicide' coupled with 'Quicksand' was released in 1974 and 'Suffragette City' coupled with 'Stay' was released in 1976 to coincide with the compilation album *ChangesOneBowie*. This single credits the A-side as being from the compilation album as opposed to *The Rise And Fall Of Ziggy Stardust And The Spiders From Mars*.

Tour Dates

Please be aware that the following list may not be exhaustive. Conflicting accounts exist of Bowie's tour dates. Consequently, the list here is derived from corroboration of information from posters, ticket stubs and reviews.

1972

22nd – 28th January	Royal Ballroom, London, England (rehearsals)
29th January	Friars Club, Borough Assembly Hall, Aylesbury, England (warm up show)
3rd February	Lancaster Arts Festival, Coventry, England (cancelled)
10th February	Tolworth, Fox At The Toby Jug, London, England
11th February	Town Hall, High Wycombe, England
12th February	Essen Pop Carnival, Grugahalle, Germany (cancelled)
12th February	Imperial College, Great Hall, London, England
23rd February	Public Hall, Wallington, England
25th February	Avery Hill College, Eltham, South London, England
26th February	Belfray Hotel, Sutton Coldfield, England
28th February	Glasgow City Hall, Glasgow, Scotland (cancelled)
29th February	Locarno Hall, Sunderland, England
1st March	Bristol University, Bristol, England
4th March	Guildhall, Portsmouth, England
7th March	Yeovil College, Yeovil, England
11th March	Guildhall, Southampton, England
14th March	Chelsea Village, Bournemouth, England
17th March	Town Hall, Birmingham, England
21st March	Free Trade Hall, Manchester, England (cancelled)
24th March	Mayfair Ballroom, Newcastle upon Tyne, England
17th April	Civic Hall, Gravesend, England (cancelled)
20th April	The Playhouse, Harlow, England
21st April	Free Trade Hall, Manchester, England
29th April	Town Hall, High Wycombe, England (cancelled)
30th April	Guildhall, Plymouth, England
3rd May	Aberystwyth University, Aberystwyth, Wales
6th May	Kingston Polytechnic, London, England
7th May	Pavilion, Hemel Hempstead, England
11th May	Assembly Hall, Worthing, England
12th May	Central Polytechnic, London, England
13th May	Technical College, Slough, England
19th May	Oxford Polytechnic, Oxford, England
20th May	Oxford Polytechnic, Oxford, England
25th May	Chelsea Village, Bournemouth, England
27th May	Ebbisham Hall, Epsom, England
2nd June	City Hall, Newcastle upon Tyne, England
3rd June	Stadium, Liverpool, England
4th June	Public Hall, Preston, England
6th June	St George's Hall, Bradford, England
7th June	City Hall, Sheffield, England
8th June	Town Hall, Middlesbrough, England
10th June	Leicester Polytechnic, Leicester, England (cancelled)
13th June	Colston Hall, Bristol, England

17th June	Town Hall, Oxford, England
19th June	Civic Hall, Southampton, England
21st June	Civic Hall, Dunstable, England
24th June	Civic Hall, Guildford, England
25th June	Fox At The Greyhound, Croydon, England
30th June	Royal Grammar School, High Wycombe, England (cancelled)
1st July	Winter Gardens, Weston-super-Mare, England
2nd July	Rainbow Pavilion, Torquay, England
8th July	Royal Festival Hall, London, England
14th July	King's Cross Cinema, London, England
15th July	Friars Club, Borough Assembly Hall, Aylesbury, England
1st-14th August	Theatre Royal Stratford East, London, England (rehearsals for Rainbow Theatre)
16th-18th	Rainbow Theatre, London, England (rehearsals)
19th August	Rainbow Theatre, London, England
20th August	Rainbow Theatre, London, England
27th August	Locarno Centre, Electric Village, Bristol, England
30th August	Rainbow Theatre, London, England
31st August	Starkers, Royal Ballroom, Bournemouth, England
1st September	Top Rank Suite, St Leger Festival, Doncaster, England
2nd September	Hard Rock, Manchester, England
3rd September	Hard Rock, Manchester, England
4th September	Top Rank Suite, Liverpool, England
5th September	Top Rank Suite, Sunderland, England
6th September	Top Rank Suite, Sheffield, England
7th September	Top Rank Suite, Stoke-on-Trent, England
22nd September	Public Hall, Cleveland, USA
24th September	Ellis Auditorium, Memphis, USA
28th September	Carnegie Hall, New York, USA
29th September	Kennedy Centre, Washington, USA
1st October	Boston Music Hall, Boston, USA
7th October	Public Auditorium, Chicago, USA
8th October	Fisher Theatre, Detroit, USA
10th October	Kiel Auditorium, St Louis, USA
11th October	Kiel Auditorium, St Louis, USA
15th October	Memorial Hall, Kansas City, USA
20th October	Santa Monica Civic Auditorium, Santa Monica, USA
21st October	Santa Monica Civic Auditorium, Santa Monica, USA
27th October	Winterland Auditorium, San Francisco, USA
28th October	Winterland Auditorium, San Francisco, USA
31st October	Paramount Theatre, Seattle, USA
1st November	Paramount Theatre, Seattle, USA
4th November	Celebrity Theatre, Phoenix, USA
5th November	Celebrity Theatre, Phoenix, USA (cancelled)
11th November	Majestic Theatre, Dallas, USA (cancelled)
12th November	Houston Music Hall, Houston, USA (cancelled)
13th November	Oklahoma City, USA (cancelled)
14th November	Loyola University, New Orleans, USA
17th November	Pirate's Cove Amusement Park, Fort Lauderdale, USA
20th November	Municipal Auditorium, Nashville, USA
22nd November	The Warehouse, New Orleans, USA
25th November	Entertainment Arena, Cleveland, USA
26th November	Entertainment Arena, Cleveland, USA
28th November	The Stanley Theatre, Pittsburgh, USA
30th November	Tower Theatre, Upper Darby, USA

1st December	Tower Theatre, Upper Darby, USA
2nd December	Tower Theatre, Upper Darby, USA
23rd December	Rainbow Theatre, London, England
24th December	Rainbow Theatre, London, England
28th December	Hard Rock, Manchester, England
29th December	Hard Rock, Manchester, England

1973

5th January	Greens Pavilion, Glasgow, Scotland
6th January	Empire Theatre, Edinburgh, Scotland
7th January	City Hall, Newcastle upon Tyne, England
9th January	Guildhall, Preston, England
19th-25th January	Royal Ballroom, Tottenham, England (rehearsals)
6th-12th February	RCA Studios, New York, USA (rehearsals)
13th February	Radio City Music Hall, New York, USA (rehearsal)
14th February	Radio City Music Hall, New York, USA
15th February	Radio City Music Hall, New York, USA
16th-20th February	Tower Theatre, Upper Darby, USA
23rd February	War Memorial Theatre, Nashville, USA
26th February	Ellis Auditorium, Memphis, USA
27th February	Ellis Auditorium, Memphis, USA
1st March	Masonic Temple Auditorium, Detroit, USA
2nd March	Masonic Temple Auditorium, Detroit, USA
3rd March	Aragon Ballroom, Chicago, USA
10th March	Long Beach Auditorium, Los Angeles, USA
11th March	Long Beach Auditorium, Los Angeles, USA
12th March	Hollywood Palladium, Los Angeles, USA
8th April	Shinjuku Koseinenkin Kaikan, Tokyo, Japan
10th April	Shinjuku Koseinenkin Kaikan, Tokyo, Japan
11th April	Shinjuku Koseinenkin Kaikan, Tokyo, Japan
12th April	Nagoya Kokusai Tenji Kaikan, Aichi, Japan
14th April	Hiroshima Yubinchokin Kaikan, Hiroshima, Japan
16th April	Kobe Kokusai Kaikan, Hyogo, Japan
17th April	Osaka Koseinenkin Kaikan, Osaka, Japan
18th April	Shibuya Kokaido, Tokyo, Japan
20th April	Shibuya Kokaido, Tokyo, Japan
8th-11th May	Central London Studios, London, England (rehearsals)
12th May	Earl's Court, London, England
16th May	Music Hall, Aberdeen, Scotland
17th May	Caird Hall, Dundee, Scotland
18th May	Greens Pavilion, Glasgow, Scotland
19th May	Empire Theatre, Edinburgh, Scotland
20st May	Theatre Royal, Norwich, England
21st May	Theatre Royal, Norwich, England
22nd May	Odeon, Romford, England
23rd May	Dome, Brighton, England
24th May	Lewisham Odeon, London, England
25th May	Winter Gardens, Bournemouth, England
27th May	Civic Hall, Guildford, England
28th May	Civic Hall, Wolverhampton, England
29th May	Victoria Hall, Hanley, Stoke-on-Trent, England
30th May	New Theatre, Oxford, England
31st May	King George's Hall, Blackburn, England

1st June	St George's Hall, Bradford, England
2nd June	Leeds University, Leeds, England (cancelled)
3rd June	New Theatre, Coventry, England
4th June	Gaumont Theatre, Worcester, England
5th June	City Hall, Sheffield, England
6th June	City Hall, Sheffield, England
7th June	Free Trade Hall, Manchester, England
8th June	City Hall, Newcastle upon Tyne, England
9th June	Guildhall, Preston, England
10th June	Empire Theatre, Liverpool, England
11th June	De Montfort Hall, Leicester, England
12th June	Central Hall, Chatham, England
13th June	Gaumont Theatre, Kilburn, London, England
14th June	City Hall, Salisbury, England
15th June	Odeon, Taunton, England
16th June	Town Hall, Torquay, England
18th June	Colston Hall, Bristol, England
19th June	Guildhall, Southampton, England (cancelled)
21st June	Town Hall, Birmingham, England
22nd June	Town Hall, Birmingham, England
23rd June	Gliderdome, Boston, England (cancelled)
24th June	Fairfield Halls, Croydon, England
25th June	New Theatre, Oxford, England
26th June	New Theatre, Oxford, England
27th June	Top Rank Suite, Doncaster, England
28th June	Royal Spa Pavilion, Bridlington, England
29th June	Rolarena, Leeds, England
30th June	Newcastle City Hall, Newcastle upon Tyne, England
2nd July	Hammersmith Odeon, London, England
3rd July	Hammersmith Odeon, London, England